The Art of Capacity Planning

SECOND EDITION

Scaling Web Resources in the Cloud

Arun Kejariwal and John Allspaw

Beijing · Boston · Farnham · Sebastopol · Tokyo

The Art of Capacity Planning

by Arun Kejariwal and John Allspaw

Printed in the United States of America.

Published by O'Reilly Media, Inc., 1005 Gravenstein Highway North, Sebastopol, CA 95472.

O'Reilly books may be purchased for educational, business, or sales promotional use. Online editions are also available for most titles (*http://oreilly.com/safari*). For more information, contact our corporate/institutional sales department: 800-998-9938 or *corporate@oreilly.com*.

Editors: Brian Anderson and Virginia Wilson
Production Editor: Nicholas Adams
Copyeditor: Octal Publishing, Inc.
Proofreader: Kim Cofer

Indexer: Ellen Troutman-Zaig
Interior Designer: David Futato
Cover Designer: Karen Montgomery
Illustrator: Rebecca Demarest

September 2008:   First Edition
October 2017:   Second Edition

Revision History for the Second Edition
2017-09-21:   First Release

See *http://oreilly.com/catalog/errata.csp?isbn=9781491939208* for release details.

978-1-491-93920-8

[LSI]

TABLE OF CONTENTS

Preface

PRIOR TO THE 2014 FIFA WORLD CUP, ONE OF THE COMMON STORIES BEING discussed at Twitter was how the service routinely became unavailable during the previous FIFA World Cup. In particular, every time Brazil or Japan scored a goal in their matches, the spike in the tweet volume used to take down the service. The *Fail Whale* (shown below) had become popular with the availability issues during the early days of Twitter. So, one of the goals for the 2014 FIFA World Cup was to have absolutely zero downtime. Further, another key goal was to ensure high performance of the Twitter mobile app—sharing photos or the like should be blazingly fast. How does one go about achieving that?

Akin to the preceding anecdote, with the increasing use of Twitter during mega events such as the Super Bowl, another key emphasis was to ensure high availability in spite of traffic—tweets, retweets, favorites, DMs—spikes. Conceivably, we can analyze the magnitude of the past spikes relative to the normal traffic and then come up with a first-cut estimate of the magnitude of the spike going forward. Having said that, should you deploy capacity to handle such one-time events, particularly given that the capacity would most likely be underutilized for most of the year? How do you handle unplanned events such as the power failure that occurred during Super Bowl XLVII in 2013? Ensuring high availability during such events calls for a systematic approach toward architectural design and capacity planning.

Capacity planning has been around since ancient times, with roots in everything from economics to engineering. In a basic sense, capacity planning is resource management. When resources are finite and come at a cost, you need to do some capacity planning. When a civil engineering firm designs a new highway system, it's planning for capacity, as is a power company planning to deliver electricity to a metropolitan area. In some ways, their concerns have a lot in common with web operations; many of the basic concepts and concerns can be applied to all three disciplines.

Although systems administration has been around since the 1960s, the branch focused on serving websites is still emerging. A large part of web operations is capacity planning and management. Those are *processes*, not *tasks*, and they are composed of many different parts. Although every organization goes about it differently, the basic concepts are the same:

- Ensure that proper resources (servers, storage, network, etc.) are available to handle expected and unexpected loads
- Have a clearly defined procurement and approval system in place

- Be prepared to justify capital expenditures in support of the business

- Have a deployment and management system in place to manage the resources after they are deployed

Why We Wrote and Revised This Book

One of the common frustrations of engineers in an operations organization and of software developers is not having somewhere to turn for help when figuring out how much capacity is needed to keep the website or mobile app running. Existing books on the topic of computer capacity planning were focused on the mathematical *theory* of resource planning, rather than the practical *implementation* of the entire process (refer to Appendix C). Further, in an Agile environment, which is a norm today, capacity planning is a continuous process and should be flexible and adaptive to the situation at hand. Basing capacity planning on static theoretical models would be a recipe for failure.

A lot of literature addressed only rudimentary models of website use cases, and lacked specific information or advice. Instead, they tended to offer mathematical models designed to illustrate the principles of queuing theory, which is the foundation of traditional capacity planning. This approach might be mathematically interesting and elegant (it also can be useful in determining what magnitude of a traffic spike can be "absorbed" by the various services, owing to built-in queues, without affecting the availability of a website/mobile app), but it doesn't help an operations engineer or a software developer when informed that he has a week to prepare for some unknown amount of additional traffic—perhaps due to the launch of a super new feature—or seeing the site dying under the weight of a link from Facebook, the *New York Times*, Reddit, Digg, and so on.

We've found most books on web capacity planning were written with the implied assumption that concepts and processes found in nonweb environments such as manufacturing or industrial engineering applied uniformly to website environments, as well. Even though some of the theory surrounding such planning might indeed be similar, the practical application of those concepts doesn't map very well to the short timelines of website development. In most web development settings, it's been our observation that change happens too fast and too often to allow for the detailed and rigorous capacity investigations common to other fields. By the time an operations engineer or a software developer comes up with the queuing model for her system, new code is deployed and the usage characteristics have likely already changed dramatically. In a 2016 Association for Computing Machinery (ACM) article titled "Why Google Stores Billions of Lines of Code in a Single Repository," authors R. Potvin and J. Levenberg (both of Google) mentioned the following:

> On a typical workday, they commit 16,000 changes to the codebase, and another 24,000 changes are committed by automated systems.

Alternatively, if some other technological, social, or real-world event occurs, it can potentially make the modeling and simulations irrelevant.

What we've found to be far more helpful, is talking to colleagues in the industry— people who encounter many of the same scaling and capacity issues. Over time, we've had contact with many different companies, each employing diverse architectures, and each experiencing different problems. But quite often they shared very similar approaches to solutions. Our hope is that we can illustrate some of these approaches in this book. The computing landscape has undergone a sea change since the writing of the first edition of this book. Cloud computing was nascent back in 2009; currently, public clouds such as AWS and Azure have grown to businesses of more than $10 billion each. Consequently, not much attention was laid on topics such as autoscaling in the first edition. In a similar vein, public clouds today offer a much larger variety of instance types, including graphics processing units (GPUs) and field-programmable gate array (FPGA)–based instances—although this is beneficial to drive higher operational efficiency, the task of "optimal" selection of an instance type for a given service has become more challenging. The growth of public clouds to new geographic regions, though good from a disaster-recovery perspective, has a direct impact on capacity planning because you need to account for tasks related to, for example, replication and load balancing.

Back in 2009, Service-Oriented Architecture (SOA) had minimal adoption, and microservices were not on the horizon. As of this writing, *serverless* is the new kid in town. The interplay between the different microservices and third-party services has a direct impact on the capacity planning process. Besides this, a lot of work has been done in the context of tooling. Given all of this, it was about time to write the second edition of this book.

Last but not least, with new websites and mobile apps springing up every day, there's always something new in the world of web operations. Consequently, the field has been thriving and conferences such as O'Reilly Velocity and Fluent serve as great forums for folks in the industry to share their insights with the community. In addition, blogs serve as a great resource to learn from the experience of others. Several papers have been written on a multitude of topics related to systems, tools, optimization and methodologies for benchmarking, and so on. To this end, among others, two key additions in the second edition are the "Readings" and "Resources" sections at the end of each chapter. These sections provide a rich source of information if you want to dive deeper into a particular subject.

Focus and Topics

This book is not about building complex models and simulations, nor is it about spending time running benchmarks over and over. It's not about mathematical concepts such as Little's Law,[1] Markov chains, or Poisson arrival rates.

What this book is about is *practical* capacity planning and management that can take place in the real world. It's about using real tools and being able to adapt to changing usage on a website that will (hopefully) grow over time. When you have a flat tire on the highway, you could spend a lot of time trying to figure out the cause, or you can get on with the obvious task of installing the spare and getting back on the road. This is the approach we are presenting to capacity planning: adaptive, not theoretical. Keep in mind a good deal of the information in this book will seem a lot like common sense —this is a good thing. Quite often the simplest approaches to problem solving are the best ones, and capacity planning is no exception. This book covers the process of capacity planning for growing websites, including measurement, procurement, and deployment. We'll discuss some of the more popular and proven measurement tools and techniques. And toward that end, we have kept the discussion platform-agnostic.

Of course, it's beyond the scope of this book to cover the details of every database, web server, caching server, and storage solution. Instead, we'll use examples of each to illustrate the process and concepts. The intention is to be as generic as possible when it

---

1 Little, J. D. C. (1961). *A Proof for the Queuing Formula: L = λW*.

comes to explaining resource management—it's the process itself we want to emphasize. For example, a database is used to store data and provide responses to queries. Most of the more popular databases allow for replicating data to other servers, which enhances redundancy, performance, and architectural decisions. It also assists the technical implementation of replication with Postgres, Oracle, or MySQL (a topic for other books). This book covers what replication means in terms of planning capacity and deployment.

Essentially, this book is about measuring, planning, and managing growth for a web application, regardless of the underlying technologies one chooses.

Audience for This Book

This book is for systems, storage, database, and network administrators; software developers; engineering managers; and, of course, capacity planners.

It's intended for people who hope (or perhaps fear) their website or mobile app will grow like those of Facebook, Instagram, Snap, WhatsApp, YouTube, Twitter, and others—companies that underwent the trial-by-fire process of scaling up as their usage skyrocketed. The approaches in this text come from real experience with sites for which traffic has grown both heavily and rapidly. If you expect the popularity of your site or app will increase dramatically the amount of traffic, please read this book.

Organization of the Material

Chapter 1, *Goals, Issues, and Processes in Capacity Planning*, presents the issues that arise over and over on heavily trafficked websites.

Chapter 2, *Setting Goals for Capacity*, illustrates the various concerns involved with planning for the growth of a web app and how capacity fits into the overall picture of availability and performance.

Chapter 3, *Measurement: Units of Capacity*, discusses capacity measurement and monitoring.

Chapter 4, *Predicting Trends*, explains how to turn measurement data into robust (i.e., not susceptible to anomalies) forecasts and how trending fits into the overall planning process.

Chapter 5, *Deployment*, discusses concepts related to deployment: automation of installation, configuration, and management.

Chapter 6, *Autoscaling*, discusses concepts related to autoscaling in the cloud.

Appendix A, *Virtualization and Cloud Computing*, discusses where virtualization and cloud services fit into a capacity plan.

Appendix B, *Dealing with Instantaneous Growth*, offers insight into what you can do in capacity crisis situations, and some best practices for dealing with site outages.

Appendix C, *Capacity Tools*, is an annotated list of measurement, installation, configuration, and management tools highlighted throughout the book.

Conventions Used in This Book

The following typographical conventions are used in this book:

Italic
  Indicates new terms, URLs, filenames, Unix utilities, and command-line options.

`Constant width`
  Indicates the contents of files, the output from commands, and generally anything found in programs.

`Constant width bold`
  Shows commands or other text that should be typed literally by the user, and parts of code or files highlighted to stand out for discussion.

`Constant width italic`
  Shows text that should be replaced with user-supplied values.

O'Reilly Safari

 *Safari* (formerly Safari Books Online) is a membership-based training and reference platform for enterprise, government, educators, and individuals.

Members have access to thousands of books, training videos, Learning Paths, interactive tutorials, and curated playlists from over 250 publishers, including O'Reilly Media, Harvard Business Review, Prentice Hall Professional, Addison-Wesley Professional, Microsoft Press, Sams, Que, Peachpit Press, Adobe, Focal Press, Cisco Press, John Wiley & Sons, Syngress, Morgan Kaufmann, IBM Redbooks, Packt, Adobe Press, FT Press, Apress, Manning, New Riders, McGraw-Hill, Jones & Bartlett, and Course Technology, among others.

For more information, please visit *http://oreilly.com/safari*.

Using Code Examples

This book is here to help you get your job done. In general, you may use the code in this book in your programs and documentation. You do not need to contact us for permission unless you're reproducing a significant portion of the code. For example, writing a program that uses several chunks of code from this book does not require permission. Selling or distributing a CD-ROM of examples from O'Reilly books *does* require permission. Answering a question by citing this book and quoting example code does not require permission. Incorporating a significant amount of example code from this book into a product's documentation *does* require permission.

We appreciate, but do not require, attribution. An attribution usually includes the title, author, publisher, and ISBN. For example: "*The Art of Capacity Planning, Second Edition* by Arun Kejariwal and John Allspaw. Copyright Arun Kejariwal, John Allspaw, 978-0-596-51857-8."

If you feel your use of code examples falls outside of fair use or the permission given above, feel free to contact us at *permissions@oreilly.com*.

We'd Like to Hear from You

Please address comments and questions concerning this book to the publisher:

O'Reilly Media, Inc.

1005 Gravenstein Highway North

Sebastopol, CA 95472

800-998-9938 (in the United States or Canada)

707-829-0515 (international or local)

707-829-0104 (fax)

We have a web page for this book, where we list errata, examples, and any additional information. You can access this page at: *http://bit.ly/the-art-of-capacity-planning-2e*

To comment or ask technical questions about this book, send email to:

bookquestions@oreilly.com

For more information about our books, conferences, Resource Centers, and the O'Reilly Network, see our website at:

http://www.oreilly.com

Acknowledgments

We would like to thank Virginia Wilson for her help with the editing and for coordinating the technical review process. Also, we would like to thank Brian Anderson for jump-starting the writing of this—the second edition—book. Thanks to Bryce Yan, Charles Border, and Coburn Watson for the technical review.

Most importantly, Arun would like to thank his wife, Pallavi Pharkya, for being understanding of the absence during the writing of this book. Likewise, John would like to thank his wife, Elizabeth Kairys, for her encouragement and support in this insane endeavor.

## CHAPTER ONE

Goals, Issues, and Processes in Capacity Planning

This chapter is designed to help you assemble and use the wealth of tools and techniques presented in the following chapters. If you do not grasp the concepts introduced in this chapter, reading the remainder of this book will be like setting out on the open ocean without knowing how to use a compass, sextant, or GPS device—you can go around in circles forever.

Background

The first edition of the book was written at the time when the use of public clouds was about to take off. Today, public clouds such as Amazon Web Services (AWS) and Microsoft Azure are businesses that generate more than $10 billion. In April 2016, IDC forecasted that the spending on IT infrastructure for cloud environments will grow to $57.8 billion in 2020. Further, the landscape of development and operations has undergone a sea change; for example, the transition from *monolithic applications* to Service-Oriented Architectures (SOAs) to *containerization* (e.g., Docker, CoreOS, Rocket, and Open Container Initiative) of applications. Likewise, another paradigm that is gaining momentum is *serverless architectures*. As per Martin Fowler:

> *Serverless architectures refer to applications that significantly depend on third-party services (knows as Backend as a Service or "BaaS") or on custom code that's run in ephemeral containers (Function as a Service or "FaaS"), the best-known vendor host of which currently is AWS Lambda. By using these ideas, and by moving much behavior to the frontend, such architectures remove the need for the traditional "always on" server system sitting behind an application. Depending on the circumstances, such systems can significantly reduce operational cost and complexity at a cost of vendor dependencies and (at the moment) immaturity of supporting services.*

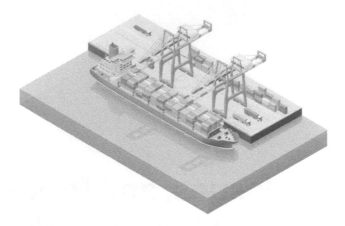

Further, the explosion of mobile traffic—as per Cisco, mobile data traffic will grow at a compound annual growth rate (CAGR) of 53 percent between 2015 and 2020, reaching 30.6 exabytes (EB) per month by 2020—and the virality of social media since the first edition has also had ramifications with respect to capacity planning. The global footprint of today's datacenters and public clouds, as exemplified by companies such as Amazon, Google, Microsoft, and Facebook, also have direct implications on capacity planning. Having said that, the concepts presented in the first edition of this book (for example, but not limited to, hardware selection, monitoring, forecasting, and deployment) are still applicable not only in the context of datacenters but also apply even in the cloud.

Preliminaries

When we break them down, capacity planning and management—the steps taken to organize the resources a site needs to run properly—are, in fact, simple processes. You begin by asking the question: what performance and availability does my organization need from the website? The answer to the former is not static; in other words, the expected performance is ever increasing owing to the progressively decreasing attention span of the end user, as illustrated in Figure 1-1 (several studies have been carried out that underscore the impact of website performance on business; see "Resources" on page 22). Having said that, you should assess the performance expected by the end user in the short term going forward. Note that meeting the expected performance is a function of, say, the type (smartphones, smart watches, tablets, etc.) of next-generation devices and the availability and growth in volume of digital media and information. The expected availability also plays a key role in the capacity planning process. We can ascribe this, in part, to aspects such as Disaster Recovery (DR), failover, and so on.

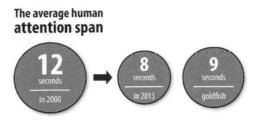

Figure 1-1. *Decreasing human attention span*

Figure 1-2 illustrates a typical modern web app, which could be a website, or one or more RESTful web APIs, or a job running in the background. A web API can be consumed either by browser clients or by native client applications or by server-side applications. As one would note from the figure, there are many components on the backend, such as a cache, a persistent data storage, a queue, a search and an authentication service, etc. Providing high availability and performance calls for, amongst other things, a systematic and robust capacity planning of each service/microservice on the backend.

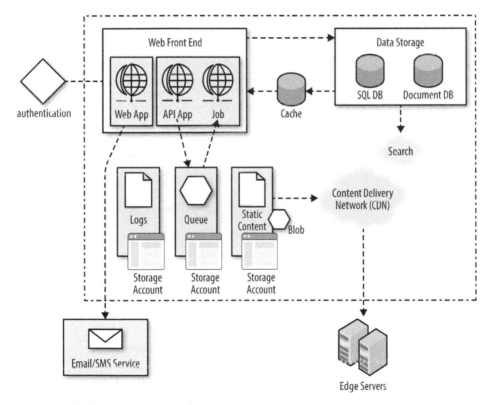

Figure 1-2. *Architecture of a typical modern web app*

First, define the application's overall load and capacity requirements using *specific* metrics, such as response times, consumable capacity, and *peak-driven processing*. Peak-driven processing is the workload experienced by an application's resources (web servers, databases, etc.) during peak usage. For instance, peak usage is exemplified by the spike in the number of tweets/minute during the Super Bowl or by the launch of a new season of *House of Cards* on Netflix. The process for determining how much capacity is needed, illustrated in Figure 1-3, involves answering the following questions:

How well is the current infrastructure working?

> Measure the characteristics of the workload for each piece of the architecture, be it in the datacenter or in the cloud, that comprise an application—web server, database server, network, and so on—and compare them to what you came up with for the aforementioned performance requirements.

What does one need in the future to maintain acceptable performance?

> Predict the future based on what one knows about growth in traffic, past system performance (note that system performance does not scale linearly with increasing traffic), and expected performance from the end user. Then, marry that prediction with what you can afford as well as a realistic timeline. Determine *what* you would need and *when* you would need it.

How can you install and manage the resources after procurement?

> Deploy this new capacity with industry-proven tools and techniques.

Rinse, repeat.

> Iterate and calibrate the capacity plan over time.

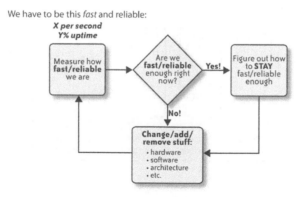

Figure 1-3. *The process for determining how much capacity is needed*

The ultimate goal lies between not buying enough hardware and wasting money on too much hardware. As functionalities are moved from hardware to software, as exemplified by Software-Defined Networking (SDN), you should include such software components in the capacity-planning process.

Let's suppose that one is a supermarket manager. One of the tasks is to manage the schedule of cashiers. A challenge in this regard is picking the appropriate number of cashiers that should be working at any moment. Assign too few, the checkout lines will become long and the customers will become irate. Schedule too many working at once and you would end up spending more money than necessary. The trick is finding the precise balance.

Now, think of the cashiers as servers, and the customers as client browsers. Be aware some cashiers might be better than others, and each day might bring a different number of customers. Then, you need to take into consideration that the supermarket is getting more and more popular. A seasoned supermarket manager intuitively knows these variables exist and attempts to strike a good balance between not frustrating the customers and not paying too many cashiers.

Welcome to the supermarket of web operations.

Quick and Dirty Math

The ideas we've just presented are hardly new, innovative, or complex. Engineering disciplines have always employed back-of-the-envelope calculations; the field of web operations is no different. In this regard, a report[1] from McKinsey reads as follows:

> But just because information may be incomplete, based on conjecture, or notably biased does not mean that it should be treated as "garbage." Soft information does have value. Sometimes, it may even be essential, especially when people try to "connect the dots" between more exact inputs or make a best guess for the emerging future.

Because we're looking to make judgments and predictions on a quickly changing landscape, approximations will be necessary, and it's important to realize what that means in terms of limitations in the process. Being aware of when detail is needed and when it's not is crucial to forecasting budgets and cost models. Unnecessary detail can potentially delay the capacity planning process, thereby risking the website/mobile apps'

---

1 "Making data analytics work for you—instead of the other way around" (2016) *http://bit.ly/making-analytics-work*

performance. Lacking the proper detail can be fatal—both from a capital expenditure (capex) and end-user experience perspective.

When operating in the cloud, you are particularly susceptible to lack of details owing to the ease of horizontal scaling and autoscaling (in Chapter 6, we detail why it is not trivial to set up autoscaling policies). Selection of "heavyweight" instance types and over-provisioning—a result of poor due diligence—are two common reasons for a fast burn rate. The article "The Three Infrastructure Mistakes Your Company Must Not Make" (*http://firstround.com/review/the-three-infrastructure-mistakes-your-company-must-not-make/*) highlighted that using a public cloud service becomes very pricey at scale. In contrast to Netflix, many other big companies—such as, but not limited to, Dropbox—that had their infrastructure on a public cloud from the beginning, have migrated to their own datacenter(s). The author of the article provides guidance when to move from a public cloud to running your own infrastructure.

Even in the context of datacenters, errors made in capacity planning due to lack of detail can have severe implications. This, in part, stems from the long supply-chain cycles and the overhead associated with provisioning and configuration. In contrast, the elasticity of the cloud, independent of cost concerns, greatly reduces the reliability risks of under-provisioning for peak workloads.

If you're interested in a more formal or academic treatment of the subject of capacity planning, refer to "Readings" on page 21.

Predicting When Systems Will Fail

Knowing when each piece of the infrastructure will fail (gracefully or not) is crucial to capacity planning. Failure in the current context can correspond to either violation of Service-Level Agreements (SLAs) (discussed further in Chapter 2), graceful degradation of performance, or a "true" system failure (determining the limits corresponding to the latter is discussed in detail in Chapter 3). Capacity planning for the web or a mobile app, more often than we would like to admit, looks like the approach shown in Figure 1-4.

Figure 1-4. *Finding failure points*

Including the information about the point of failure as part of the calculations is mandatory, not optional. However, determining the limits of each portion of a site's backend can be tricky. An easily segmented architecture helps you to find the limits of the current hardware configurations. You then can use those capacity ceilings as a basis for predicting future growth.

For example, let's assume that you have a database server that responds to queries from the frontend web servers. Planning for capacity means knowing the answers to questions such as these:

- Taking into account the specific hardware configuration, how many queries per second (QPS) can the database server manage?
- How many QPS can it serve before performance degradation affects end-user experience?

Adjusting for periodic spikes and subtracting some comfortable percentage of headroom (or safety factor, which we talk about later) will render a single number with which you can characterize that database configuration vis-à-vis the specific role. On finding that "red line" metric, you will know the following:

- The load that will cause the database to be unresponsive or, in the worst case, failover, which will allow you to set alert thresholds accordingly.
- What to expect from adding (or removing) similar database servers to the backend.
- When to begin sizing another order of new database capacity.

We talk more about these last points in the coming chapters. One thing to note is the entire capacity planning process is going to be *architecture-specific*. This means that the calculations that you make to predict increasing capacity might have other constraints specific to a particular application. For example, most (if not all) large-scale internet services have an SOA or microservice architecture (MSA), each microservice being containerized. In an SOA setting, capacity planning for an individual service is influenced by other upstream and downstream services. Likewise, the use of virtual machine (VM) versus container instances or the adoption of a partial serverless system architecture (*http://martinfowler.com/articles/serverless.html*) has direct implications on capacity planning.

For example, to spread out the load, a LAMP application (LAMP standing for Linux, Apache, MySQL, PHP5) might utilize a MySQL server as a master database in which all live data is written and maintained. We might use a second, replicated slave database for read-only database operations. Adding more slave databases to scale the read-only traffic is generally an appropriate technique, but many large websites have been forthright about their experiences with this approach and the limits they've encountered. There is a limit to how many read-only slave databases you can add before you begin to realize diminishing returns as the rate and volume of changes to data on the master database might be more than the replicated slaves can sustain, no matter how many are added. This is just one example of how an architecture can have a large effect on your ability to add capacity.

Expanding database-driven web applications might take different paths in their evolution toward scalable maturity. Some might choose to federate data across many master databases. They might split the database into their own clusters, or choose to cache data in a variety of methods to reduce load on their database layer. Yet others might take a hybrid approach, using all of these methods of scaling. This book is not intended to be an advice column on database scaling; it's meant to serve as a guide by which you can come up with your own planning and measurement process—one that is suitable for your environment.

Make System Stats Tell Stories

Server statistics paint only part of the picture of a system's health. Unless you can tie them to actual site or mobile app metrics, server statistics don't mean very much in terms of characterizing usage. And this is something you would need to know in order to track how capacity will change over time.

For example, knowing that web servers are processing X requests per second is handy, but it's also good to know what those X requests per second actually mean in terms of number of users. Maybe X requests per second represents Y number of users employing the site simultaneously.

It would be even better to know that of those Y simultaneous users, A percent *are live streaming an event*, B percent are uploading photos/videos, C percent are making comments on a heated forum topic, and D percent are poking randomly around the site/mobile app while waiting for the pizza guy to arrive. Measuring those user metrics over time is a first step. Comparing and graphing the web server hits-per-second against those user interaction metrics will ultimately yield some of the cost of providing service to the users. In the preceding examples, the ability to generate a comment within the application might consume more resources than simply browsing the site, but it consumes less when compared to uploading a photo. Having some idea of which features tax the capacity more than others gives you the context in which to decide where you would want to focus priority attention in the capacity planning process. These observations can also help drive any technology procurement justifications. A classic example of this is the Retweet feature in Twitter. A retweet by a celebrity such as Lady Gaga strains the service severely owing to the large fan out (which corresponds to a large number of followers—as of January 21, 2017, Lady Gaga had 64,990,626 followers!) and the virality effect.

Spikes in traffic are not limited to social media. Traffic spikes are routinely observed by ecommerce platforms such as Amazon, eBay, Etsy, and Shopify during the holiday season, broadcasting of ads during events such as Super Bowl, and the launch of, say, a much-awaited music album. From a business perspective, it is critical to survive these bursts in traffic. At the same time, it is not financially sound to have the capacity required to handle the traffic bursts to be always running. To this end, queuing and caching-based approaches have been employed to handle the traffic burst, thereby alleviating the capex overhead.

> ───── **NOTE** ─────────────────────────────────
>
> For a reference to a talk about flash sales engineering at Shopify, refer to "Resources" on page 22.

Spikes in capacity usage during such cases should serve as a forcing function to revisit the design and architecture of a service. This is well exemplified by the famous tweet from Ellen DeGeneres during the 2014 Oscars (see Figure 1-5), which garnered a large number of views and, more important, a large number of retweets in a short timespan. The outage that happened post Ellen's Oscar tweet was due to a combination of a missing architecture component in one of the data stores as well as the search tier. Proper load testing of the scenario—more than a million people search for the same tweet and then retweet it—would have avoided the outage.

Quite often, the person approving expensive hardware and software requests is not the same person making the requests. Finance and business leaders must sometimes trust implicitly that their engineers are providing accurate information when they request capital for resources. Tying system statistics to business metrics helps bring the technology closer to the business units, and can help engineers understand what the growth means in terms of business success. Marrying these two metrics together can therefore help spread the awareness that technology costs shouldn't automatically be considered a cost center, but rather a significant driver of revenue. It also means that future capital expenditure costs have some real context so that even those nontechnical folks will understand the value technology investment brings.

If only Bradley's arm was longer. Best photo ever. #oscars

Figure 1-5. *A tweet whose retweeting induced an outage*

For example, when you're presenting a proposal for an order of new database hardware, you should have the systems and application metrics on hand to justify the investment. If you had the pertinent supporting data, you could say something along the following lines:

> *...And if we get these new database servers, we'll be able to serve our pages* X *percent faster, which means our pageviews—and corresponding ad revenues—have an opportunity to increase up to* Y *percent.*

The following illustrates another way to make a business case for a capex request:

> *The A/B test results of product P demonstrate an X% uptick in click-through rate, which we expect to translate to an increase in Y dollars on a quarterly basis or an approximate Z% increase in revenue after worldwide launch. This justifies the expected capex of C dollars needed for the launch of P worldwide.*

The cost of having extra capacity headroom should be justified by correlating it with avoidance of risk associated with not having the capacity ready to go if and when there is a spike in traffic. In the event of a pushback from the finance folks, you should highlight the severity of adverse impact on the user experience due to the lack of investment and the consequent impact on the bottom line of the business. Thus, capacity planning entails managing risk to the business.

Backing up the justifications in this way also can help the business development people understand what success means in terms of capacity management.

Measure, Measure, Measure

Engineers like graphs for good reason: they tell a story better than numbers can by themselves and let you know exactly how the system is performing. There are some industry-tested tools and techniques used in measuring system statistics, such as CPU, memory, load, and disk usage. You can reuse a lot of them to measure anything you need, including application-level or business metrics.

Another theme in this book is measurement, which should be considered a necessity, not an option. There's a fuel gauge on your car's dashboard for a reason. Don't make the mistake of not installing one on your systems. We look at this in more detail in Chapter 3.

Be it capacity or any other context under the operations umbrella, it is not uncommon to observe localized efforts toward planning and optimization, which limits their impact on the overall business. In this regard, in their book titled *The Goal: A Process of Ongoing Improvement* (North River Press), Goldratt and Cox present a very compelling walkthrough, using a manufacturing plant as an example, of how to employ a business-centric approach toward developing a process of ongoing improvement. (Refer to "Readings" on page 21 for other suggested references.) Following are the key pillars of business-centric capacity planning:

- What is the goal for capacity planning?
  - Deliver the best end-user experience because it is one of the key drivers for both user acquisition and user retention.
    - Meet well-defined performance, availability, and reliability targets (SLAs are discussed in Chapter 2).
    - Support organic growth and launch of new features or products.
    - Note that the goal in and of itself should not be to reduce the operational footprint or improve resource utilization (discussed further in Chapter 2

and Chapter 3). Datacenter or cloud efficiency is unquestionably important because it directly affects operating expense (opex); having said that, efforts geared toward optimizing opex should not adversely affect the aforementioned goal.

- Understanding the following concepts:
  — Dependent events
      ○ Chart out the interactions between the different components—for instance, services or microservices—of the underlying architecture.

   ○ Determine the key bottleneck(s) with respect to the high-level goal. Bottlenecks can be induced due to a wide variety of reasons such as presence of a critical section (for references to prior research work on the topic, refer to "Readings" on page 21). In a similar vein, bottleneck(s) can assume many different forms such as low throughput at high resource utilization,[2] lack of fault tolerance, and small capacity headroom. When finding the bottlenecks, you should focus on the root cause, not the effects. It is important to keep in mind that the high-level goal is always subject to the bottleneck(s) only.

   Note that bottlenecks are not limited to one or more services or microservices. Suppliers in a supply chain also can be a bottleneck toward achieving the high-level goal. Thus, procurement (and deployment) are integral steps in the capacity planning process.

   ○ In practice, characteristics of an application evolve on an ongoing basis owing to an Agile development environment coupled with dynamic incoming user traffic. For instance, the dependencies between different microservices can change over time. This potentially can give rise to new

---

2 A potential root cause can be ascribed to, but not limited to, poor selection of algorithm/data structure(s) or poor implementation.

bottleneck(s), and existing bottleneck(s) might be masked. This in turn would directly affect the capacity planning process. Exposing this to finance and business leaders is critical to having them appreciate the need for revising the capacity plan that was presented the last time.

o Note that the higher the dependencies between the different components, the higher the complexity of the system and, consequently, the higher probability of cascading of potential capacity issues from one component to another.

— Statistical fluctuations

o How do endogenous and/or exogenous factors—such as a new release or loss of a server in case of the former or events such as the Olympics or Super Bowl in case of the latter—affect the high-level goal and the capacity headroom of each component? For instance, typically, the capacity headroom of bottlenecks is highly susceptible to incoming traffic.

o To what extent can the increase in input traffic be absorbed—for instance, via queuing—by each component? Further, given that not all the incoming traffic is of equal "importance"—for example, searching for a celebrity versus the list of survivors during an earthquake—it is important to support priority scheduling for the queues associated with the bottleneck(s).

o How to address—for example, by setting up graceful degradation—the trade-off between capacity headroom and queuing for each component without affecting the high-level goal. Note that consuming the capacity headroom helps to drain the queue; however, it risks not being able to serve a high volume and high-priority traffic going forward. In contrast, maintaining a healthy capacity headroom at the expense of queuing can potentially result in violation of SLAs.

• Being agile in the presence of conflicting requests and changing priorities

— For instance, in the context of web search, improving the freshness and ranking exercises pressure on the crawler and ranking components respectively of a web search engine. Given a fixed capex budget, the requirements of the afore-mentioned components for additional capacity might conflict with one another. This, in and of itself, can potentially be de-prioritized in the wake of capacity required to, for instance, support the launch of a new product.

— It's not uncommon to have policies set up to address the aforementioned cases. However, more than often, such policies do not serve their purpose. This can be attributed, in part, to a) policies are, by definition, not malleable to the constantly changing ground realities in production, and b) a bureaucratic framework inevitably grows around such policies, which in turn builds inertia and slows down the decision-making process.

• Working in close collaboration with product and engineering teams

— This is critical so as to be able to assess the capacity requirements going forward. Given the long lead times in procurement, it is of utmost importance to be predictive not reactive about one's capacity requirements going forward. Even in the context of cloud computing wherein you can spin up new instances in a matter of a few minutes, it is important—for both startups and public companies—to keep a tab on one's expected opex going forward. Further, an understanding of the product and engineering roadmaps can assist in hardware selection (we discuss this further in Chapter 3).

— Given that in most cases the milestones on the roadmaps of different product and engineering teams are not aligned and that the capacity requirements differ from one team to another, procurement of different elements of the infrastructure should be pipelined in a capacity plan. In addition, you can go a step further by pipelining the procurement of different pieces of hardware (e.g., drives, memory, network switches, etc.).

A poor capacity plan can result in, for example, missing a deadline or a lost opportunity with respect to user acquisition or retention, which in turn has a direct impact on the bottom line of the business. As pointed out by Goldratt and Cox, "optimal" decision-making is a synchronized effort of people across (possible) multiple teams, not driven by policies.

As businesses evolve in an increasingly connected world, the complexities of applications will grow, as well. This coupled with increasing rate of innovation, being able to plan ahead well is going to be (as it is even now) a key contributor to success and growth of a business. To this end, as argued by Goldratt and Cox, *thinking processes* that trigger new ideas to solve problems associated with emerging applications need to be developed. Broadly speaking, the thinking processes cater to the following three fundamental questions:

- What to change?
- What to change to?
- How to cause the change?

These questions provide a general framework to address an unforeseen problem. Having said that, as mentioned earlier, you should always relate the problem at hand with the high-level business goal. This ensures that you're not mired in a local optimum and that every action or decision is geared toward achieving the goal.

Buying Stuff

After you have completed all the measurements, made estimations about usage, and sketched out predictions for future requirements, you need to actually buy things: bandwidth, storage or storage appliances, servers, maybe even *instances* of virtual servers or containers in the cloud. In each case, you would need to explain to the people with the checkbooks why your enterprise needs these things and when. (We talk more about predicting the future and presenting those findings in Chapter 4.)

In the cloud context, you can add capacity—be it compute and memory, network bandwidth, or storage—with the push of a button. You can use multicloud Continuous Delivery (CD) platforms such as Spinnaker (*http://www.spinnaker.io/*) for this. Having said that, proper due diligence is called for so as to avoid under-provisioning or over-provisioning. At Netflix, which is based entirely on AWS, engineers provision on-demand, putting in place effective cost reporting mechanisms at the team level to provide feedback on capacity growth. In general, this can potentially land you in—as put forward by Avi Freedman—a *cloud jail*, wherein you find yourself spending far too much money on infrastructure and are completely beholden to a cloud provider. The latter stems from the fact that you're using the specific services and environments of the cloud provider. It's not easy and is very expensive to switch after this happens.

Procurement is a process, and it should be treated as yet another part of capacity planning. Whether it's a call to a hosting provider to bring new capacity online, a request for quotes from a vendor, or a trip to a local computer store, you need to take this important segment of time into account. Smaller companies, although usually a lot less "liquid" than their larger brethren, can really shine in this arena. Being small often goes hand-in-hand with being nimble. So, even though you might not be offered the best price on equipment as the big companies who buy in massive bulk, you would likely be able to get it faster, owing to a less cumbersome approval process.

The person you probably need to persuade is the CFO, who sits across the hall. In the early days of Flickr, we used to be able to get quotes from a vendor and simply walk over to the founder of the company (seated 20 feet away), who could cut and send a check. The servers would arrive in about a week, and we would rack them in the data-center the day they came out of the box. Easy!

Amazon, Yahoo!, Twitter, Google, Microsoft, and other big companies with their own datacenters have a more involved cycle of vetting hardware requests that includes obtaining many levels of approval and coordinating delivery to various datacenters around the world. After purchases have been made, the local site operations teams in each datacenter then must assemble, rack, cable, and install operating systems on each of the boxes. This all takes more time than for a startup. Of course, the flip side is that at a large company, you can take advantage of buying power. By buying in bulk, organizations can afford more hardware, at a better price. In either case, the concern is the same: the procurement process should be baked into a larger planning exercise. It takes time and effort, just like all the other steps. (We discuss this more in Chapter 4.)

Performance and Capacity: Two Different Animals

The relationship between performance tuning and capacity planning is often misunderstood. Although they affect each other, they have different goals. Performance tuning optimizes the *existing* system for better performance. Capacity planning determines what a system needs and when it needs it, using the current performance as a baseline.

Common Sense Steps and Methods

Real-world observations are worth more than any theoretical measurement. Capacity planning—and the predictions that drive it—should come from the *empirical* observation of a site's usage, not benchmarks made in artificial environments.

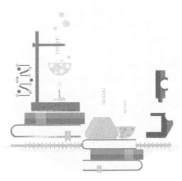

For example, the SPEC CPU2006 benchmark suite (*http://spec.org/cpu2006/*), in spite of being more than 10 years old, is still used for comparative measurement of compute-intensive performance across the widest practical range of hardware using workloads developed from real user applications. However, based on workload analysis, we find that, almost always, the characteristics of the benchmarks in the suite are very different from web applications. Consequently, basing hardware selection on SPECspeed and/or SPECrate metrics would skew the decision-making and, in the worst case, have adverse implications on the business. Recently, SPEC announced the Cloud IaaS 2016 suite (*http://spec.org/cloud_iaas2016/*). The suite is designed to stress provisioning as well as runtime aspects of a cloud using I/O- and CPU-intensive cloud computing workloads. The suite comprises of the social media NoSQL database transaction and K-Means clustering using map/reduce as two significant and representative workload types within cloud computing. In practice, the representativeness of the two workloads is very limited because the production workloads span a much wider spectrum of workload types.

Benchmarking and performance research have value, but you shouldn't use them as the sole indicators of capacity.

Let's face it: tuning is fun and addictive. But after you spend some time tweaking values, testing, and tweaking some more, it can become an endless hole, sucking away time and energy for little or no gain. There are those rare and beautiful times when you stumble upon some obvious and simple parameter that can make everything faster—you come across the one MySQL configuration parameter that doubles the cache size, or realize after some testing that those TCP window sizes set in the kernel can really make a difference. Great! But, as illustrated in Figure 1-6, for each of those rare gems we discover, the number of obvious optimizations we find thereafter dwindles pretty rapidly. After claiming the low-hanging fruits, the marginal benefit of employing sophisticated techniques—compiler-driven code optimizations, profile-guided optimization, dynamic optimization, and so on—does not often merit the required investment of time. In such scenarios, high-level optimizations, which often entail system or algorithmic redesign, are warranted to squeeze out further performance gain, if any!

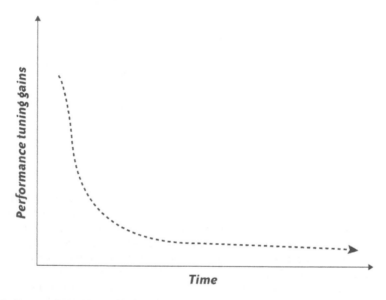

Figure 1-6. *Decreasing returns from performance tuning*

Capacity planning must happen *without* regard to what you might optimize. The first real step in the process is to accept the system's *current* performance in order to estimate what you might need in the future. If at some point down the road you discover some tweak that brings about more resources, that's a bonus.

Here's a quick example of the difference between performance and capacity. Suppose that there is a butcher in San Francisco who prepares the most delectable bacon in the state of California. Let's assume that the butcher shop has an arrangement with a store in San Jose to sell their great bacon there. Every day, the butcher needs to transport the bacon from San Francisco to San Jose using some number of trucks—and the bacon must get there within an hour. The butcher needs to determine what type of trucks he'll need and how many of them to get the bacon to San Jose. The demand for the bacon in San Jose is increasing with time. It's difficult having the best bacon in the state, but it's a good problem to have.

The butcher has three trucks that suffice for the moment. But he knows that he might be doubling the amount of bacon he'll need to transport over the next couple of months. At this point, he need to do one of two things:

- Make the trucks go faster
- Get more trucks

You're probably beginning to see the point here. Even though the butcher might squeeze some extra horsepower out of the trucks by having them tuned up—or by convincing the drivers to exceed the speed limit—he's not going to achieve the same efficiency gain that would come from simply purchasing more trucks. He has no choice but to accept the performance of each truck and then work from there.

The moral of this little story? When faced with the question of capacity, try to ignore those urges to make existing gear faster; instead, focus on the topic at hand, which is finding out what your enterprise needs, and when.

One other note about performance tuning and capacity: there is no silver bullet formula that we can pass on to you as to when tuning is appropriate and when it's not. It might be that simply buying more hardware and spinning up new instances in the cloud is the correct thing to do when weighed against engineering time spent on tuning the existing system. This is exemplified by a sudden spike in the number of transactions on an ecommerce website or app owing to a sale or a spike in the number of searches on Google after an incident such as an outbreak of a disease. Almost always, events that can potentially affect end-user experience adversely (which in turn affects the bottom line) warrant immediate scaling up of the capacity and foregoing performance optimization. On the other hand, performance tuning is of high importance for startups as they need to minimize their opex costs, which in part helps to keep a check on their burn rate. Striking this balance between optimization and capacity deployment is a challenge and will differ from environment to environment.

The Effects of Social Websites and Open APIs

As more and more websites install Web 2.0 characteristics, web operations are becoming increasingly important, especially capacity management. If a site contains content generated by its users, utilization and growth isn't completely under the control of the site's creators—a large portion of that control is in the hands of the user community. In a similar vein, the capacity requirements are also governed by the use of third-party vendors for key services such as, but not limited to, managed DNS, content delivery, content acceleration, adserving, analytics, behavioral targeting, content optimization, and widgets. Further, in the age of social media, the incoming traffic is also subject to virality effects. This can be scary for people accustomed to building sites with very predictable growth patterns, because it means capacity is difficult to predict and needs to be on the radar of all those invested, both the business and the technology staff. The challenge for development and operations staff of a social website is to stay ahead of the growing usage by collecting enough data from that upward spiral to drive informed planning for the future.

Architecture and Its Effect on Capacity

The way you drive your car affects its mileage. We can apply a similar principle to web architectures. One of the recurring themes in this book will be how a website's architecture can have a significant impact on how we use, consume, and manage capacity. Design has greater effect on the effective use of capacity than any tuning and tweaking of the servers and the network. Design also plays a large role in how easily and flexibly you can add or subtract capacity as the need arises.

Although software and hardware tuning, optimization, and performance tweaking are related to capacity planning, they are not the same thing. This book focuses on tuning an architecture to allow for easier capacity management. Keeping the pieces of an architecture easily divisible and segmented—as exemplified by SOAs or, more recently, the increasing emphasis on containerization of services—can help you to tackle a lot of load characterization problems, problems you would need to solve before you can create an accurate picture of what will be required to grow, and when.

Providing web services via open APIs (e.g., APIs exposed by Ad exchanges, Twitter's API, Facebook's Atlas/Graph/Marketing APIs) introduces another ball of wax altogether, given that an application's data will be accessed by yet more applications, each with their own usage and growth patterns. It also means users have a convenient way to abuse the system, which puts more uncertainty into the capacity equation. API usage needs to be monitored to watch for emerging patterns, usage edge cases, and rogue application developers bent on crawling the entire database tree. A classic example of the latter is illustrated by attempts to scrape the connections of LinkedIn's website. Controls need to be in place to enforce the guidelines or Terms of Service (TOS), which should accompany any open API web service (more about that in Chapter 3).

In John's first year working at Flickr, photo uploads grew from 60 per minute to 660. Flickr expanded from consuming 200 GB of disk space per day to 880, and then ballooned from serving 3,000 images a second to 8,000. And that was just in the first year. Today, internet powerhouses have dozens of datacenters around the globe. In fact, as per Gartner (*http://www.gartner.com/technology/research/it-spending-forecast/*), in 2016, the worldwide spending on datacenter systems is expected to top $175 billion and the overall IT spending is expected to be in the order of $3.4 trillion.

Capacity planning can become very important, very quickly. But it's not all that difficult; all you need to do is pay a little attention to the right factors. The rest of the chapters in this book will show you how to do this. We'll split up this process into segments:

- Determining the goals (Chapter 2)
- Collecting metrics, finding the limits, and hardware selection (Chapter 3)
- Plotting out the trends and making robust (i.e., not susceptible to anomalies) forecasts based on those metrics and limits (Chapter 4)
- Deploying and managing the capacity (Chapter 5)
- Managing capacity in the cloud via autoscaling (Chapter 6)

Readings

1. D. A. Menascé et al. *Performance by Design: Computer Capacity Planning by Example.*

2. N. J. Gunther. *Guerrilla Capacity Planning.*

3. R. Cammarota et al. (2014). *Pruning Hardware Evaluation Space via Correlation-driven Application Similarity Analysis.*

4. K. Matthias and S. P. Kane. *Docker: Up & Running: Shipping Reliable Containers in Production.*

5. A. Mouat. *Using Docker: Developing and Deploying Software with Containers.*

6. K. Hightower. *Kubernetes: Up and Running.*

7. E. M. Goldratt and J. Cox. *The Goal: A Process of Ongoing Improvement.*

8. G. Kim et al. *The Phoenix Project: A Novel About IT, DevOps, and Helping Your Business Win Kindle Edition.*

Critical Section

1. E. W. Dijkstra. (1965). *Solution of a problem in concurrent programming control.*

2. L. Lamport. (1974). *A new solution of Dijkstra's concurrent programming problem.*

3. G. L. Peterson and M. J. Fischer. (1977). *Economical solutions for the critical section problem in a distributed system* (Extended Abstract).

4. M. Blasgen et al. (1977). *The Convoy Phenomenon.*

5. H. P. Katseff. (1978). *A new solution to the critical section problem.*

6. L. Lamport. (1986). *The Mutual Exclusion Problem: Part I – A Theory of Interprocess Communication.*

7. L. Lamport. (1986). *The Mutual Exclusion Problem: Part II – Statement and Solutions.*

Resources

1. "Cloud Environments Will Drive IT Infrastructure Spending Growth Across All Regional Markets in 2016, According to IDC." (2016) *http://bit.ly/idc-cloud-env.*

2. "Cisco Visual Networking Index: Forecast and Methodology, 2016–2021." (2017) *http://bit.ly/cisco-vis-net.*

3. M. Costigan. (2016). *Risk-based Capacity Planning.*

4. "Risk-Based Capacity Planning." (2016) *http://ubm.io/2h85HKL.*

5. "You Now Have a Shorter Attention Span Than a Goldfish." (2017) *http://ti.me/2wnVOQv.*

6. L. Ridley. (2014). *People swap devices 21 times an hour, says OMD* (*http://www.campaign live.co.uk/article/people-swap-devices-21-times-hour-says-omd/1225960*).

7. B. Koley. (2014). *Software Defined Networking at Scale* (*https://research.google.com/pubs/pub42948.html*).

8. "Scaling to exabytes and beyond." (2016) *https://blogs.dropbox.com/tech/2016/03/magic-pocket-infrastructure/.*

9. "Mitigating Risks through Capacity Planning to achieve Competitive Advantage." (2013) *http://india.cgnglobal.com/node/47*.

10. "The Epic Story of Dropbox's Exodus from the Amazon Cloud Empire." (2016) *https://www.wired.com/2016/03/epic-story-dropboxs-exodus-amazon-cloud-empire/*.

11. "Speed Matters for Google Web Search." (2009) *http://services.google.com/fh/files/blogs/google_delayexp.pdf*.

12. "Cedexis Announces Impact, Connects Website Performance To Online Business Results." (2015) *http://www.cedexis.com/blog/cedexis-announces-impact-connects-website-performance-to-online-business-results/*.

13. "How Loading Time Affects Your Bottom Line." (2011) *https://blog.kissmetrics.com/loading-time/*.

14. "Speed Is A Killer – Why Decreasing Page Load Time Can Drastically Increase Conversions." (2011) *https://blog.kissmetrics.com/speed-is-a-killer/*.

15. "Why Web Performance Matters: Is Your Site Driving Customers Away?" (2010) *http://bit.ly/why-web-perf*.

16. "Why You Need a Seriously Fast Website." (2013) *http://www.copyblogger.com/website-speed-matters/*.

17. "Monitor and Improve Web Performance Using RUM Data Visualization." (2014) *http://bit.ly/mon-improve-web-perf*.

18. "The Importance of Website Loading Speed & Top 3 Factors That Limit Website Speed." (2014) *http://bit.ly/importance-load-speed*.

19. "Seven Rules of Thumb for Web Site Experimenters." (2014) *http://stanford.io/2wsXzKJ*.

20. "SEO 101: How Important is Site Speed in 2014?" (2014) *http://www.searchengine journal.com/seo-101-important-site-speed-2014/111924/*.

21. "User Preference and Search Engine Latency." *http://bit.ly/user-pref-search*.

22. "Flash Sale Engineering." (2016) *https://www.usenix.org/conference/srecon16europe/program/presentation/stolarsky*.

23. "How micro services are breaking down the enterprise monoliths." (2016) *http://www.appstechnews.com/news/2016/nov/16/micro-services-breaking-down-monolith/*.

24. "Breaking Down a Monolithic Software: A Case for Microservices vs. Self-Contained Systems." (2016) *http://bit.ly/breaking-down-monolith*.

25. "Breaking a Monolithic API into Microservices at Uber." (2016) *https://www.infoq.com/news/2016/07/uber-microservices*.

26. "What's Your Headroom?" (2016) *http://akamai.me/2x5a3eR*.

## CHAPTER TWO

Setting Goals for Capacity

You wouldn't begin mixing concrete before you know what you're building. Similarly, you shouldn't begin planning for capacity before you determine the requirements for performance, availability, and reliability of a site or mobile app. As Chapter 1 mentions, the requirements change as the end user's expectations evolve. The requirements are also a function of the technology; for example, use of virtual machines (VMs) versus use of containers. Consequently, capacity planning is not a one-time process, but a continuous one.

Capacity planning involves a lot of assumptions related to why your enterprise needs the capacity. Some of these assumptions are obvious, whereas others are not. For example, if you don't know that you *should* be serving the pages in less than three seconds, you're going to have a tough time determining how many servers will be needed to satisfy that requirement. More important, it will be even tougher to determine how many servers you would need to add as the traffic grows.

Common sense, right? Yes, but it's amazing how many organizations don't take the time to assemble a rudimentary list of operational requirements. Waiting until users complain about slow responses or time-outs isn't a good strategy.

Establishing the acceptable speed or reliability of each part of the site can be a considerable undertaking, but it will pay off when you're planning for growth and need to know what standard you should maintain. This chapter shows you how to understand the different types of requirements the management and customers will force you to deal with, and how architectural design helps with this planning.

Different Kinds of Requirements and Measurements

Now that we're talking about requirements—which might be set by others, external to your group—we can look at the different types you would need to deal with. The managers, the end users, and the clients running websites all have varying objectives and measure success in different ways. Even in the serverless context (*http://martin fowler.com/articles/serverless.html*), you must specify the Service-Level Agreement (SLA) or Service-Level Objectives (SLO) requirements for the service being used so that you can meet your own performance targets or SLAs (discussed later in this chapter). Ultimately, these requirements, or capacity goals, are interrelated and can be distilled into the following:

- Performance, availability, and reliability
  - External service monitoring
  - Business requirements
  - User expectations
- Capacity
  - System metrics
  - Resource ceilings

External Service Monitoring

A site or mobile app should be available not only to your colleagues performing tests on the website from a facility down the road, but also to real visitors who might be located on other continents with slow connections. This is particularly important given that the speed of mobile networks varies significantly around the globe, which is illustrated in Figure 2-1.

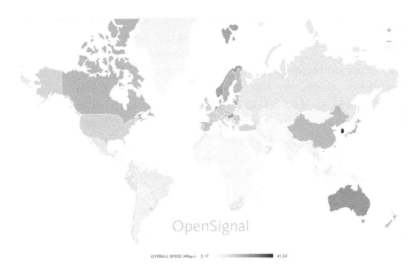

Figure 2-1. *Speed of mobile networks around the globe (source: https://opensignal.com/reports/2016/08/global-state-of-the-mobile-network/)*

Likewise, the density of feature phones and the different generations of smartphones —say, iPhone 4 versus iPhone 5 versus iPhone 6 versus iPhone 7—varies significantly around the globe. Performance sensitivity of users of old generation phones is much higher than that of users of new generation phones. To this end, companies such as Facebook are testing stripped-down versions of their apps for lower-end phones.

Some large companies choose to have site performance (and availability) constantly monitored by services such as Catchpoint (*http://catchpoint.com/*), Keynote (*http://keynote.com/*), Gomez (*http://gomez.com/*), and Soasta (*http://soasta.com/*). These commercial services deploy worldwide networks of machines that constantly ping the web pages to record the response time and a variety of other metrics such as the following:

- Domain Name Server (DNS) time
- Secure Sockets Layer (SSL) time
- Wire time
- Wait time
- Time to first byte (TTFB)
- Page load time
- Time to render start
- Above-the-fold (AFT) time
- Document completion time

The service providers keep track of all these metrics and build handy-dandy dashboards to evaluate how the site performance and uptime appears from many locations around the world. Because the aforementioned third parties are deemed "objective," the statistics reported by them can be used to enforce or guide SLAs arranged with partner companies or sites (we talk more about SLAs later). Keynote and Gomez can be considered enterprise-level services. There are also plenty of low-cost alternatives, including PingDom (*http://pingdom.com/*), SiteUptime (*http://siteuptime.com/*), and Alertra (*http://alertra.com/*). Having visibility into the aforementioned metrics—preferably in the form of intelligent alerts—can help expose potential capacity issues. In light of the explosion in the number of metrics being collected nowadays, carrying visual analysis to detect anomalies is no longer practical. Further, visual analysis is error prone. A large number of false positives would result in alert fatigue. Hence, one should carry out anomaly detection algorithmically.

It's important to understand exactly what these services measure and how to interpret the numbers they generate. Because most of them are networks of *machines* rather than people, it's essential to be aware of how those web pages are being requested. Some things to consider when you're looking at a monitoring service include the following:

- Are they simulating human users?

  The intent of the users has a direct impact on their interaction with a website or a mobile app. For instance, in the context of search, the following types of intent have been reported in prior research:

  — Navigational

  — Informational

  — Commercial

  — Transactional

In a similar vein, how users interact with the content—primarily images and video —on a web page or in an app has direct ramifications on their online experiences. User settings such as whether *Location Services, Notifications,* and *Limit Ad Tracking* (a feature in iOS 10) are turned on or off determine the amount of data that an app can collect, which in turn affects the responsiveness of a mobile app.

Thus, it is critical to understand how the monitoring services model behavior and how reflective their model is of your typical end user.

- Are they caching objects like a normal web browser would? Why or why not?

  Recall that all modern browsers support caching. Having said that, cache size differs between a desktop browser and a mobile browser. Further, caching is not ubiquitous in the mobile app world. In the context of user acquisition (UA), you should plan for the worst-case scenario; that is, assume a *cold cache.*

- Can you determine how much time is spent due to network transfer versus server time, in the aggregate as well as for each object?

- Can you determine whether a failure or unexpected wait time is due to geo graphic network issues, server-side issues, or measurement failures?

  For example, guaranteeing consistency—the desired level differs on a case-by-case basis—in a distributed database or a distributed warehouse (as exemplified by Google's Spanner and Mesa, respectively) often induces a performance penalty or can affect availability. Likewise, an unexpected wait time might stem from an issue with one or more network load balancers.

To address these questions, you would need to go through the documentation of the monitoring service. If it's not clear from the documentation, you should reach out to the architect or technical lead of the service. If you think that the service monitoring systems are testing in a manner representative of the users when they visit the site, you have good reason to trust the numbers. Also keep in mind, the metrics you use for capacity planning or site performance measurement might ultimately find their way onto an executive dashboard somewhere, viewed by a nontechnical audience.

CFOs, CTOs, business development folks, and even CEOs can become addicted to qualitative assessments of operations. This can be a double-edged sword. On the one hand, you are being transparent about failures, which can help when you're attempting to justify expenditures and organizational changes to support capacity. On the other hand, you also are giving a frequently obsessive crowd more to obsess about, so when there are any anomalies in this data—for example, such as long response times due to failures or sudden surge in traffic—you should be prepared to explain what they mean.

SLAs

So, what exactly is an SLA? It's an instrument that makes business people comfortable, much like insurance. But in broader, less anxious terms, an SLA is a metric that defines how a service should operate within agreed-upon boundaries. It puts some financial muscle into the metric by establishing a schedule of credits for meeting goals, or possibly penalties if the service does not achieve them. With websites, SLAs cover mostly *availability* and *performance*. Thus, SLAs directly influence architectural design and the capacity planning process.

Some SLAs guarantee that a service will be available for a preestablished percentage of time, such as 99.99 percent. What this means is that 0.01 percent of the time, the service can be unavailable, and it will still be within the bounds of the SLA. Other SLAs require that demand for a service stay within reasonable limits; request rate limits or storage and upload limits are typical parameters.

For example, you might find a web hosting company that uses verbiage similar to the following in its "Terms of Service" document:

> *Acme Hosting, Inc. will use commercially reasonable efforts to make the SuperHosting-Plan available with a monthly uptime percentage (defined below) of at least 99.9% during any monthly billing cycle. In the event Acme Hosting, Inc. does not meet this commitment, you will be eligible to receive a service credit as described here:*

Monthly uptime percentage	Credit percentage
Between 99 and 99.9%	1 day credit
Less than 99%	1 week credit

Looks pretty reassuring, doesn't it? The problem is, 99.9 percent uptime stretched over a month isn't as great a number as you might think:

- 30 days = 720 hours = 43,200 minutes
- 99.9 percent of 43,200 minutes = 43,156.8 minutes
- 43,200 minutes − 43,156.8 minutes = 43.2 minutes

This means for 43.2 minutes every month, this service can go down without penalty. If the site generates $3,000 worth of sales every minute, you could easily calculate how much money any amount of downtime will cost (along with the less measurable consequence of disgruntled customers). Table 2-1 shows percentages of uptime on a yearly basis.

Table 2-1. *SLA percentages and acceptable downtimes*

Uptime SLA	Downtime per year
90.0 percent	36 days, 12 hours
95.0 percent	18 days, 6 hours
99.0 percent	87 hours, 36 minutes
99.50 percent	43 hours, 48 minutes
99.90 percent	8 hours, 45 minutes, 36 seconds
99.99 percent	52 minutes, 33 seconds
99.999 percent	5 minutes, 15 seconds
99.9999 percent	32 seconds

The term *five-nines* is commonly heard in discussions about SLAs and availability. This refers to 99.999 percent availability and it is used in marketing literature at least as much as it is in technical literature. Five-nines is usually used to indicate the site or system is deemed to be *highly* available. The table includes uptime percentages other than the ones discussed earlier. It's not uncommon for operations folks to use 95 percent and *two-nines* and *four-nines*.

These SLA availability numbers aim to provide not only a level of confidence in a website's service, but also imply that you can equate downtime to lost revenue. We don't believe that this is actually accurate, because the straight math will bear out. If the service is unavailable for 10 minutes and it normally produces $3,000 of revenue every minute, you might assume the business has lost $30,000. In reality, customers might just pick up where they left off and buy what they were in the process of buying when the outage occurred. The business might be spending extra money on the customer service side to make up for an outage that has no impact on the earnings.

──── NOTE ──

For further discussion of the revenue impact on performance, refer to *http://blog.catchpoint.com/2017/01/06/performance-impact-revenue-real/*.

The point is, while the analysis of the financial impact of an outage might be neither true nor accurate, the importance of availability should be clear.

Business Capacity Requirements

The use of *web services* is becoming more and more prevalent in today's Web 3.0 mashup-y and mobile app world. Although most web services and platforms offer open APIs (e.g., Facebook's Graph API and Twitter's Streaming APIs) for individual application developers to build upon, business-to-business relationships depend on them, as well. Therefore, companies usually tie revenue streams to having unfettered access to an API. This could mean a business relationship relies on a certain level of availability, or performance of the API, measured in a percentage uptime (such as 99.99 percent) and/or an agreed-upon rate of API requests.

Let's assume that a website provides postal codes, given various inputs to the API that you have built. You might allow only one API call per minute to a regular or noncommercial user, but a shipping company might enter into a contract permitting it to call the API up to 10 times per *second*. In the context of social media, the numbers corresponding to the user base and traffic are much higher. For example, the statistics in Figure 2-2 were posted by Jan Koum (cofounder of WhatsApp) on Facebook on February 1, 2016.

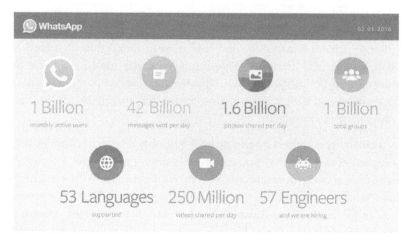

Figure 2-2. *WhatsApp user base and traffic as of February 1, 2016 (source: http://bit.ly/2vLGoEs)*

Likewise, as of 26 April, 2017, Instagram has more than 700 million Monthly Active Users (MAUs),[1] over 400 million Daily Active Users (DAUs), and more than 95 million photos/videos are uploaded on Instagram on a daily basis. Supporting such high and, more important, growing traffic calls for very systematic capacity planning. Website capacity planning is as much about justifying capital expenditures as it is about technical issues, such as scaling, architectures, software, and hardware. Because capacity concerns can have such a large impact on *business* operations, they should be considered early in the process of development.

User Expectations

Obviously, the end goal of capacity planning is a smooth and speedy experience for the users. User expectations vary depending on what type of application they are using and even what portion of the application they are interacting with. For example, the expectation for speed when searching for vacation packages on a travel site is different than it is for loading the checkout page.

It is well known that the perceived performance of a website or mobile app directly affects user engagement. To this end, several metrics have been proposed to quantify perceived performance:

- First paint
- Render start
- DOM interactive
- Speed index
- AFT time
- Object rendering time (aka Hero image timing)
- Critical resources

---

1 "700 Million." *http://blog.instagram.com/post/160011713372/170426-700million*

Besides the aforementioned metrics, another alternative is to use the User Timing "Standard Mark Names" such as "mark_fully_loaded," "mark_fully_visible," "mark_above_the_fold," and "mark_time_to_user_action." Different metrics capture different aspects of the user experience; hence, you should not look for a one-size-fits-all metric.

> **NOTE**
>
> For links to the discussions of the aforementioned metrics, refer to "Resources" on page 44.

It's possible to have plenty of capacity but a slow website nonetheless, and, in the worst case, the service can be unavailable. This is not uncommon today when most of the content of a web page is predominantly high-quality images or videos—the key drivers of high user engagement and conversion and potential sources of performance drag. In a similar vein, with the increasing use of third-party services, a web page can potentially become unavailable in spite of having ample capacity.

> **NOTE**
>
> Designing fast and highly available web pages is beyond the scope of this book, but you can find a lot of great information in Steve Souders' excellent book, *High Performance Web Sites* (O'Reilly) and in Ilya Grigorik's book titled *High Performance Browser Networking* (O'Reilly). To learn how to mitigate the impact on performance by rendering high-quality images and videos, check out Colin Bendell et al. *High Performance Images* (O'Reilly) and Ilya Grigorik's book *High Performance Browser Networking* (O'Reilly); the book is also available for free at *https://hpbn.co/*. To learn how to achieve high availability, refer to Lee Atchison's *Architecting for Scale: High Availability for Your Growing Applications* (O'Reilly).

Even though capacity is only one part of making the end-user experience fast, that experience is still one of the real-world metrics that we'll want to measure and track in order to make capacity forecasts. For example, when serving static web content, you might reach an intolerable amount of latency at high volumes before any system-level metrics (CPU, disk, memory) raise a red flag. Again, this can have more to do with the construction of the web page than the capacity of the servers sending the content. But because capacity is one of the more expensive pieces to change, it warrants investigation. Perceived slowness of a web page *could* be the result of a page that is simply too heavy, and not from a lack of capacity. (This is one of the fundamentals of Souders' book.) It's a good idea to determine whether this is the case when any user-perceived slowness is analyzed. The problem can be solved by either adding capacity or changing the page weight. The former can sometimes involve more cost than the latter.

Determining the root cause of the perceived slowness of a web page is, relatively speaking, easier in the context of monolithic architectures than in the context of

Service-Oriented Architecture (SOA) or microservice architecture (MSA) (Chapter 1 discusses these briefly). Services such as Twitter and Netflix comprise hundreds of microservices. In an MSA, typically each microservice provides a specific functionality; for example, at Twitter, there are different microservices for recommending "Who To Follow," revealing relevant tweets for the "While You Were Away" product feature. The complex interactions between the different microservices results in cascading of performance issues—this adversely affects Mean Time to Resolution (MTTR). Further, the use of third-party vendors for key services—such as managed DNS, content delivery, content acceleration, adserving, analytics, behavioral targeting, content optimization, and widgets—makes diagnosis of performance issues even more challenging.

When John was at Flickr, tens of thousands of photos were served per second. Each photo server could serve a known and specific rate of images before reaching its maximum. The maximum was not defined in terms of disk I/O, CPU, or memory, but in terms of how many images could be served without the "time to serve" for each image exceeding the specified amount of time.

Architecture Decisions

The architecture is the basic layout of how all of the backend pieces—both hardware and software—are joined. Its design plays a crucial role in your ability to plan and manage capacity.

NOTE

Designing the architecture can be a complex undertaking, but there are a couple of great books available on the subject: Cal Henderson's *Building Scalable Web Sites* (O'Reilly) and Theo Schlossnagle's *Scalable Internet Architectures* (Pearson). In the mobile context, take a look at Maximiliano Firtman's *High Performance Mobile Web* (O'Reilly). For developing high-performance iOS and Android apps, read Gaurav Vaish's *High Performance iOS Apps* (O'Reilly) and Doug Sillars' *High Performance Android Apps* (O'Reilly).

The architecture affects nearly every part of performance, reliability, and management. Establishing a good architecture almost always makes capacity planning easier.

Providing Measurement Points

Both for measurement purposes as well as for rapid response to changing conditions, the architecture should be designed such that you easily can split it into parts that perform discrete tasks. In an ideal world, each component of the backend should have a single job to do, but it could still do multiple jobs well, if needed. At the same time, its effectiveness on each job should be easy to measure. To this end, MSA has gained momentum in recent years. In particular, microservices are a way of developing and composing software systems such that they are built out of small, independent components that interact with one another over the network. By limiting dependencies on other parts of the system, MSAs can be changed much more quickly (as compared to their monolithic counterparts) in response to a bug or a feature request. With increasing containerization of MSAs—which is exemplified by support for containers in public clouds such as Amazon Web Services (AWS), Microsofts Azure, Google Cloud Platform (GCP), and IBM Bluemix—you can take advantage of the built-in support for monitoring in containers to measure task-level metrics.

―――― NOTE ――――――――――――――――――――――――――――――――――

For references to information on containers, go to the section "Readings" on page 44.

For instance, let's look at a simple database-driven web. To get the most bang for our buck, we have our web server and our database residing on the same hardware server. This means that all of the moving parts share the same hardware resources, as shown in Figure 2-3.

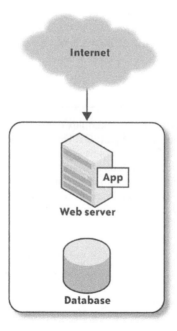

Figure 2-3. *A simple, single-server web application architecture*

Suppose that you have configured measurements for both system and application-level statistics for the server. You can measure the system statistics of this server via sar or rrdtool and application-level metrics such as web resource requests or database queries-per-second.

The difficulty with the setup in Figure 2-3 is that you can't easily distinguish which system statistics correspond with the different pieces of the architecture. Therefore, one can't answer basic questions that are likely to arise, such as:

- Is the disk utilization the result of the web server sending out a lot of static content from the disk, or are the database's queries being disk-bound?
- How much of the filesystem cache, CPU, memory, and disk utilization is being consumed by the web server, and how much is being used for the database?

With careful research, you can make some estimates about which daemon is using which resource. In the best case, the resource demands of the different daemons don't contend with one another. For example, the web server might be bound mostly by CPU and not need much memory, whereas the database might be memory-bound without using much CPU. But even in this ideal scenario, if usage continues to grow, the resource contention will grow to warrant splitting the architecture into different hardware components (Figure 2-4). The splitting enables performance isolation between the various services. At that point, you would really like to know how much CPU, cache, disk space, bus bandwidth, and so on that each daemon actually needs.

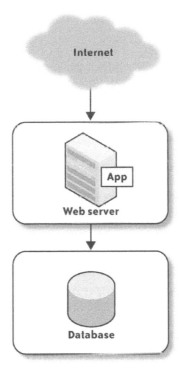

Figure 2-4. *Separation of web server and database*

Splitting the nodes in this fashion makes it easier to understand the capacity demands, given that the resources on each server are now dedicated to each piece of the architecture. It also means that you can measure each server and its resource demands more distinctly. You could come to conclusions with the single-component configuration, but with less ease and accuracy. Of course, this division of labor also produces performance gains, such as preventing frontend client-side traffic from interfering with database traffic, but let's forget about performance for the moment.

If we're recording system- and application-level statistics, we can quantify what each unit of capacity means in terms of usage. With this new architecture, we can answer a few questions that we couldn't before:

Database server
How do increases in database queries-per-second affect the following?

- Disk utilization
- I/O wait (percent of time the database waits due to network or disk operations)
- RAM usage
- CPU usage

Web server
How do increases in web server requests-per-second affect the following?

- Disk utilization
- I/O Wait
- RAM usage
- CPU usage

Being able to answer these questions is key to establishing how (and when) we would want to add more capacity to each piece.

Resource Ceilings

Now that you have a good idea of what's required for each piece of this simple architecture, you can get a sense for whether you would want different hardware configurations.

For instance, back in our days at Flickr, for the most part, our MySQL database installations happened to be disk-bound, so there was no compelling reason to buy two quad-core CPUs for each database box. Instead, we spent money on more disk spindles and memory to help with filesystem performance and caching. We knew this to be our ideal database hardware configuration—for our database. We had different configurations for our image serving machines, our web servers, and our image processing machines; all according to what in-box resources they relied on most.

The last piece we're missing in this discussion on architecture is what drives capacity forecasting: *resource ceilings*. The questions posed earlier regarding the effect of usage on resources point to an obvious culmination: *when will the database or web server die?*

Each server in our example possesses a finite amount of the following hardware resources:

- Disk throughput
- Disk storage
- CPU
- RAM
- Network

High loads will bump against the limits of one or more of those resources. Somewhere just below that critical level is where one would want to determine the *ceiling* for each piece of the architecture. The ceiling is the critical level of a particular resource (or resources) that cannot be crossed without failure or violation of one or more SLAs. Armed with the current ceilings, you can begin to assemble the capacity plan. In practice, different services exert different resource pressure. Owing to this, public clouds offer a wide range of instance types; for example, as of November 26, 2016, AWS EC2 supports more than 40 different instance types and Google Compute Engine supports more than 15 instance types. We talk more about examples of ceilings in Chapter 3.

As you can see, changing architecture in simple ways can help you to understand for what purposes the capacity is being used. When thinking about architecture design, keep in mind the division of labor and the "small pieces, loosely joined" theory can go a long way toward giving you clues regarding how the site is being used. We touch more on architecture decisions throughout the book, and particularly in Chapter 3.

Hardware Decisions (Vertical, Horizontal, and Diagonal Scaling)

Choosing the right hardware for each component of the architecture can greatly affect costs. At the very least, when it comes to servers, you should have a basic idea (gleaned from measurement and usage patterns) of where you would want to invest money. Before perusing a vendor's current pricing, be aware of what it is that you're trying to achieve. Will this server be required to do a lot of CPU work? Will it need to perform a lot of memory work? Is it a network-bound gateway?

Today, the difference between horizontal and vertical scaling architectures are quite well known in the industry, but it's worth reviewing in order to put capacity planning into context (Figure 2-5):

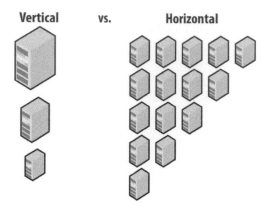

Figure 2-5. *Illustration of Vertical versus Horizontal scaling*

- Being able to scale *horizontally* means having an architecture that allows for adding capacity by simply adding similarly functioning nodes to the existing infrastructure. For instance, a second web server to share the burden of website visits. Under horizontal scaling, only the resources required to address the bottlenecks of a service need to be scaled. Horizontal scaling is the typical choice in the case of MSAs.

- Being able to scale *vertically* is the capability of adding capacity by increasing the resources internal to a server, such as CPU, memory, disk, and network. Vertical scaling is the typical choice in the case of monolithic architectures.

Since the emergence of tiered and *shared-nothing* architectures, horizontal scaling has been widely recognized for its advantages over vertical scaling as it pertains to web applications. Being able to scale horizontally means designing an application to handle various levels of database abstraction and distribution. You can find great approaches to horizontal application development techniques in the aforementioned books by Henderson and Schlossnagle.

The danger of relying *solely* on vertical scaling is that as you continue to upgrade components of a single computer, the cost rises dramatically. You also introduce the risk of a *single point of failure* (SPOF). Horizontal scaling involves the more complex issue of increasing the potential failure points as one expands the size of the server farm. In addition, one inherently introduces some challenges surrounding any synchronization one would need between the nodes. For example, guaranteeing strong consistency in a distributed database or a distributed warehouse requires synchronization between the various nodes. Likewise, in the context of multithreaded execution, thread synchronization is often needed (but not always) to guarantee correctness.

Diagonal scaling (a term coined by Arun) is the process of vertically scaling the horizontally scaled nodes that an enterprise already has in the infrastructure. Over time, CPU power and RAM become faster, cheaper, and cooler, and disk storage becomes larger and less expensive. Thus, it can be cost effective to keep some vertical scaling as part of the plan, but applied to horizontal nodes.

What this all boils down to is that for all the nodes bound on CPU or RAM, you can "upgrade" to fewer servers with more CPU and RAM. For disk-bound boxes, it also can mean that you might be able to replace them with fewer machines that have more disk spindles.

As an example, let's consider an upgrade that we did while working at Yahoo! Initially, we had 67 dual-CPU, 4 GB RAM, single SATA drive web servers. For the most part, our frontend layer was CPU-bound, handling requests from client browsers, making backend database calls, and taking photo uploads. These 67 machines were equipped with Intel Xeon 2.80 GHz CPUs running Apache and PHP. When it was time to add capacity, we decided to try the new Quad Core CPU boxes. We found the dual-quad core machines had roughly three times the processing power of the existing dual-CPU boxes. With 8 CPU cores of Intel Xeon L5320 1.86 GHz CPUs, we were able to replace 67 existing boxes with only 18 new boxes. Figure 2-6 illustrates how much the server load average (across the entire cluster) dropped as a result.

Figure 2-6 shows the reduction in load average when the 67 machines were removed from the production pool and the 18 new boxes were allowed to take over for the same production load. This certainly makes for a very dramatic-looking graph, but load average might not be the best metric to illustrate this diagonal scaling exercise.

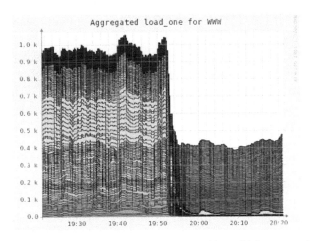

Figure 2-6. *Load average drop by replacing 67 boxes with 18 higher-capacity boxes*

Figure 2-7 represents the same time period as Figure 2-6, except that it details the number of Apache requests-per-second when the older servers were replaced. The shades of lines on the graph represent a single server, making it clear when the newer servers took over. Note that the amount of Apache requests-per-second actually went up by as much as 400 after the replacement, implying that the older machines were very close to their own bottlenecks.

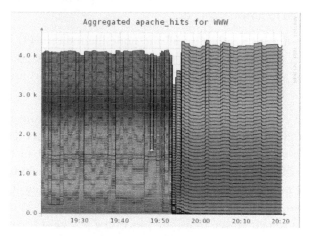

Figure 2-7. *Serving more traffic with fewer servers*

Table 2-2 shows what this meant in terms of resources.

Table 2-2. *Comparing server architectures*

Servers	CPU	RAM	Disk	Power (kW) at 60 percent of peak usage
67	2 (2 cores)	4 GB	1 x 80 GB SATA	8.763
18	2 (8 cores)	4 GB	1 x 146 GB SATA	2.332

Based on traffic patterns, if we assume that the servers are working at an average of about 60 percent of their peak, this means that we're using roughly 30 percent of the electrical power we were using previously. We've also saved 49U of rack space because each server needs only 1U of space. That's more than one full, standard 42U rack emptied as a result of diagonal scaling. Not bad.

Disaster Recovery

Disaster Recovery pertains to saving business operations (along with other resources such as data, which we won't consider in this book) after a natural or human-induced catastrophe. By catastrophe, we are not implying the failure of a single server, but a complete outage that's usually external to the operation of the website infrastructure.

Examples of such disasters include datacenter power or cooling outages as well as physical disasters such as earthquakes. It also can include incidents, such as construction accidents or explosions that affect the power, cooling, or network connectivity relied upon by the site. Regardless of the cause, the effect is the same: your enterprise can't serve the website or mobile app. Continuing to serve traffic under failure conditions is obviously an important part of web operations and architecture design. Contingency planning clearly involves capacity management. *Disaster Recovery* (DR) is only one part of what is termed *Business Continuity Planning* (BCP), which is the larger logistical plan to ensure continuity of business in the face of different failure event scenarios.

In most cases, the solution is to deploy complete architectures in two (or more) separate physical locations, which means multiplying the infrastructure costs. It also means multiplying the nodes the enterprise would need to manage, doubling all of the data replication, code, and configuration deployment, and multiplying all of the monitoring and measurement applications by the number of datacenters you deploy.

Clearly, DR plans raise both financial and technical concerns. DR and BCP are large topics in and of themselves and are beyond the scope of this book. If this topic is of particular interest to you, there are many books available—for example, Susan Snedakar's *Business Continuity and Disaster Recovery Planning for IT Professionals* (O'Reilly)— dedicated specifically to this subject.

Readings

1. T. Ruotsale et al. (2015). *Interactive Intent Modeling: Information Discovery Beyond Search (http://cacm.acm.org/magazines/2015/1/181621-interactive-intent-modeling).*

2. J. C. Corbett et al. (2013). *Spanner: Google's Globally Distributed Database.*

3. A. Gupta et al. (2016). *Mesa: A Geo-Replicated Online Data Warehouse for Google's Advertising System (http://cacm.acm.org/magazines/2016/7/204037-mesa/fulltext).*

4. D. E. Eisenbud et al. (2016). *Maglev: A Fast and Reliable Software Network Load Balancer.*

Resources

1. "Benchmarking Cassandra Scalability on AWS—Over a million writes per second." (2011) *http://techblog.netflix.com/2011/11/benchmarking-cassandra-scalability-on.html.*

2. "Mobile vs Desktop: 13 Essential User Behaviors." (2016) *http://bit.ly/mobile-vs-desktop-13.*

3. "Keywords Are Dead! Long Live User Intent!" (2013) *http://bit.ly/keywords-are-dead.*

4. "Measuring Perceived Performance." (2016) *http://bit.ly/measuring-perceived.*

5. "A Practical Guide to SLAs." (2016) *http://bit.ly/sla-practical-guide.*

6. "The Very Real Performance Impact on Revenue." (2017) *http://blog.catchpoint.com/2017/01/06/performance-impact-revenue-real/.*

7. "Performance Impact of Third Party Components." (2016) *http://blog.catchpoint.com/2016/09/23/third-party-performance-impact/.*

8. "Speed Index." *https://sites.google.com/a/webpagetest.org/docs/using-webpagetest/metrics/speed-index.*

9. "Above the Fold Time: Measuring Web Page Performance Visually." (2011) *http://bit.ly/above-the-fold-time.*

10. "Hero Image Custom Metrics." (2015) *http://bit.ly/hero-image.*

11. "Critical Metric: Critical Resources." (2016) *http://bit.ly/crit-met-crit-res.*

CHAPTER THREE

Measurement: Units of Capacity

The only man who behaves sensibly is my tailor; he takes my measurements anew every time he sees me, while all the rest go on with their old measurements and expect me to fit them.

—George Bernard Shaw

If you don't have a way to measure current capacity, you can't conduct capacity planning—you would only be guessing. Fortunately, a seemingly endless range of tools is available for measuring computer performance and usage. Most operating systems come with some basic built-in utilities that can measure various performance and resource consumption metrics. Most of these utilities usually provide a way to record results, as well. For instance, on Linux, the following commands are commonly used:

uptime

> You use this to view the load averages, which in turn indicates the number of tasks (processes) that are queued up to run. For links to the discussions about understanding uptime, go to the section "Resources" on page 100.

dmesg

> You use this to view the last 10 system messages, if there are any, and look for errors that can cause performance issues.

vmstat 1

> This provides a summary of key server statistics—such as processes running on the CPU and waiting for a turn, free memory in kilobytes, swap-ins, and swap-outs—every second.

mpstat -P ALL 1

> This provides CPU time breakdowns per CPU every second.

pistat 1

> This provides a per-process summary on a rolling basis.

iostat -xz 1

> You use this for understanding block devices (disks), both the workload applied and the resulting performance.

free -m

> You can use this to view the amount of free memory available and the size of the buffer and file cache.

sar -n DEV 1

> Use this to view the network interface throughput: rxkB/s and txkB/s, as a measure of workload and also to check whether any limit has been reached.

sar -n TCP,ETCP 1

> You can use this to view the server load in terms of the number of locally/remotely initiated TCP connections per second and the number of TCP retransmits per second.

`top`

Use this to view the summary of most of the metrics exposed by the aforementioned commands.

Other tools such as `netstat`, `tcpstat`, and `ncstat` are commonly used. Figure 3-1 presents an overview of the various tools available for Linux.

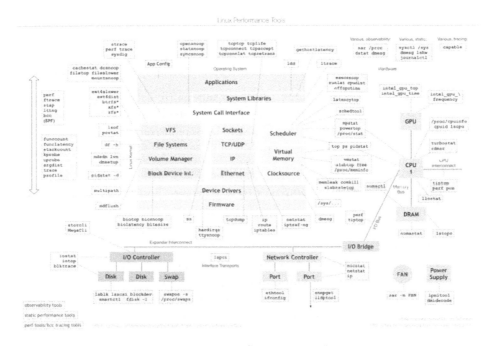

Figure 3-1. *Landscape of monitoring tools available in Linux (source: http://www.brendan-gregg.com/Perf/linux_perf_tools_full.png)*

In addition to the tools shown in Figure 3-1, there are tools that are more advanced and enable monitoring at the kernel level. For example, you can use SystemTap to extract, filter, and summarize data so that you can diagnose complex performance or functional problems of a Linux system. Using a SystemTap script, you can name events and give them handlers. Whenever a specified event occurs, the Linux kernel runs the handler as if it were a quick subroutine and then resumes. There are many other types of events such as entering or exiting a function, a timer expiring, or the entire System-Tap session starting or stopping. A handler is a series of script language statements that specify the work to be done whenever the event occurs. This work normally includes extracting data from the event context, storing the data into internal variables, or printing results.

Akin to SystemTap (stap), you also can use ktap—which is based on bytecode, so it doesn't depend upon the GNU Compiler Collection (GCC) and doesn't require compiling the kernel module for each script—for dynamic tracing of the Linux kernel. In a similar vein, Linux enhanced BPF (Berkeley Packet Filter) also has raw tracing capabilities, and you can use it to carry out custom analysis by attaching the BPF bytecode with Linux kernel dynamic tracing (kprobe), user-level dynamic tracing (uprobes), kernel static tracing (tracepoints), and profiling events. eBPF was described by Ingo Molnár (*https://lkml.org/lkml/2015/4/14/232*) as follows:

> *One of the more interesting features in this cycle is the ability to attach eBPF programs (user-defined, sandboxed bytecode executed by the kernel) to kprobes. This allows user-defined instrumentation on a live kernel image that can never crash, hang or interfere with the kernel negatively.*

Unlike other built-in tracers in Linux, eBPF can summarize data in kernel context and emits only the summary you care about to user level—for example, latency histograms and filesystem I/O. You can use eBPF in a wide variety of contexts, such as Software-Defined Networks (SDNs), Distributed Denial of Service (DDoS) mitigation, and intrusion detection.

The discussion so far has been at the host level. However, host-level monitoring is not sufficient in a virtualized or containerized environment. To this end, both virtual machines (VMs) and containers come along with tools to expose CPU, memory, I/O, and network metrics on a per–VM/container basis. Besides the standard metrics, container-specific metrics such as CPU throttling are also exposed. For instance, Docker surfaces the number of times throttling was enforced for each container, and the total time that each container was throttled. Likewise, Docker exposes a metric called container memory fail counter, which is increased each time memory allocation fails, i.e., each time the preset memory limit is hit. Thus, spikes in this metric suggest that one or more containers need more memory than what was allocated. If the process in the container terminates because of this error, you also might see out-of-memory events from Docker.

Most popular open source tools are easy to download and run on virtually any modern system. For capacity planning, the measurement tools should provide, at minimum, an easy way to do the following:

- Record and store data over time—maintaining a history is key for many reasons such as forecasting and trend analysis

- Build custom metrics

- Compare metrics from various sources such as RRD (discussed further later), Hadoop, OpenTSDB, and so on

- Import and export metrics as, for example, CSVs, JSON, and so forth

As long as you choose tools that can in some way satisfy the aforementioned criteria, you don't need to spend much time pondering which to use. What is more important is to determine which metrics to measure and which metrics to give particular attention.

Metrics have different flavors. The common case is of the form *<name/value*, timestamp>. The *name* is in the form of a k-tuple, e.g., *<hostname, process, status>*. On the other hand, values can assume the following types:

- Counter
- Gauge
- Percentiles
- Interval
- Ratio

Resolution and diversity of metrics being collected play a vital role toward effective capacity planning. For instance, in the context of the cloud, collecting metrics at hourly/daily granularity limits the triggering of an autoscaling action in a timely fashion (we discuss autoscaling in detail in Chapter 6). Likewise, lack of diversity of the metrics at disposal can potentially misguide capacity planning. Although monitoring a large set of metrics enables carrying out correlation analysis (which in turn helps to weed out false positives), it is not in and of itself reflective of diversity of the metrics.

Increase in resolution and number of metrics being collected has direct ramifications on the capital expenditure (capex) required for monitoring (refer to the sidebar "Accepting the Observer Effect") and makes analysis more challenging. The impact of the former can be contained via techniques such as downsampling, filtering, or aggregation. You should make the selection of one or more techniques on a case-by-case basis because the requirements of each user of the monitoring system often differ from one another.

It is not uncommon for the volume of metadata (associated with a metric) collected to eclipse the volume of the metric itself. This also has direct impact on the capex required for monitoring. Further, unfortunately, more than 90 percent of the metrics and the corresponding metadata collected is never read—in other words, it is never used. This indeed used to be the case at Netflix and Twitter.

> ──── **NOTE** ────────────────────────────────
>
> For a discussion of the pros and cons of some of the commonly used monitoring tools, refer to Caskey Dickson's talk at the LISA'13 conference (*https://www.usenix.org/conference/lisa13/working-theory-monitoring*).

In this chapter, we discuss the specific statistics such as cache hit rate and disk usage rate that you would want to measure for different purposes and then show the results in graphs to help you better interpret them. There are plenty of other sources of information on how to set up particular tools to generate the measurements; most professional system administrators already have such tools installed.

Accepting the Observer Effect

Measuring systems introduces yet another task a server will be asked to perform in order to function properly. Some system resources are going to be consumed for the purposes of collection and transfer of metrics. Good monitoring tools make an effort to be lightweight and not get in the way of a server's primary work, but there will always be some amount of overhead. In this regard, Arun's experience has been that for profiling a Java application, using YourKit was very intrusive, whereas using Sun Studio (even within a VirtualBox environment) was very lightweight. Low overhead is particularly important for latency-sensitive—say, less than 100 ms–applications.

This means that measuring a system's resources will in some small way (hopefully, very small) affect the system's behavior, and, by extension, the very measurements you end up recording. This is commonly known as the *observer effect*.

Our philosophy has been to accept the burden on the server and the slight distortion in the data collected as a cost of doing business. Giving up some percentage of CPU, disk, memory, and network resources to provide clear and useful measurement data is a small price to pay for monitoring a system's overall health and capacity.

Capacity Tracking Tools

This chapter is about automatically and routinely measuring server behavior over a predefined amount of time. By monitoring normal behavior over days, weeks, and months, you would be able to see both patterns that recur regularly as well as trends over time that help predict when you would need to increase capacity. The former is exemplified by an increase in traffic on Friday evenings and over the weekends; the latter is exemplified by an organic increase in traffic over a longer period (for example, three to six months). You must be wary of using data corresponding to longer periods because, in some context, data recency is key to decision making.

We also discuss deliberately increasing the load through artificial scaling (also referred to as *load testing*) using methods that closely simulate what will happen to the site under test in the future. You can use tools such as Loadrunner (*http://bit.ly/microfocus-loadrunner*), Iago (*https://github.com/twitter/iago*), or JMeter (*http://jmeter.apache.org/*) for load testing. This will also help you to predict when to increase capacity.

For the tasks in this chapter, you would need tools that collect, store, and display (usually on a graph) metrics over time. You can use them to drive capacity predictions as well as root-cause analysis.

Examples of these tools include the following:

- Cacti (*http://cacti.net*)
- Ganglia (*http://ganglia.info*)
- Graphite (*http://graphiteapp.org*)

Tools such as Grafana (*http://grafana.org*) are often used to query and visualize time-series of operational metrics. The tools don't need to be fancy. In fact, for some metrics, you can simply load them into Excel and plot them there. Appendix C contains a more comprehensive list of capacity planning tools. In similar fashion, several commercial infrastructure monitoring services have sprung to this end:

- Datadog (*http://datadog.com*)
- SysDig (*http://sysdig.com*)
- Ruxit (*https://www.dynatrace.com/platform/offerings/ruxit/*)
- LogicMonitor (*http://logicmonitor.com*)
- Sematext (*http://sematext.com*)
- CoScale (*http://coscale.com*)
- Signal FX (*http://signalfx.com*)
- Riemann (*http://riemann.io*)

- Prometheus (*http://prometheus.io*)

- Sensu (*http://sensuapp.org*)

- Idera (*http://idera.com*)

- Bijk (*http://bijk.com*)

- X-Pack (*http://elastic.co/products/x-pack/monitoring*)

- vRealize Hyperic HQ (*http://www.vmware.com/products/vrealize-hyperic.html*)

It's important to begin by understanding the types of monitoring to which this chapter refers. Companies in the web operations field use the term *monitoring* to describe all sorts of operations—generating alerts concerning system availability, data collection and its analysis, real-world (commonly referred to as RUM, real user monitoring[1]) and artificial end user interaction measurement (commonly referred to as synthetic monitoring)—the list goes on and on. Quite often this causes confusion. We suspect many commercial vendors who align on any one of those areas exploit this confusion to further their own goals, much to our detriment as end users.

This chapter is *not* concerned with system availability, the health of servers, or notification management—the sorts of activities offered by Nagios, Zenoss, OpenNMS, and other popular network monitoring systems such as Wireshark, GFI LanGuard, NetXMS, and PRTG Network Monitor. Some of these tools do offer some of the features we need for our monitoring purposes, such as the ability to display and store metrics. But they exist mostly to help recognize urgent problems and avoid imminent disasters. For the most part, they function a lot like extremely complex alarm clocks and smoke detectors.

Metric collection systems, on the other hand, act more like court reporters, who observe and record what's going on without taking any action whatsoever. As it pertains to our goals, the term "monitoring" refers to metric collection systems used to collect, store, and display system- and application-level metrics of an infrastructure.

Fundamentals and Elements of Metric Collection Systems

Nearly every major commercial and open source metric collection system employs the same architecture. As depicted in Figure 3-2, this architecture usually consists of an *agent* that runs on each of the physical machines being monitored, and a single *server* that aggregates and displays the metrics. As the number of nodes in an infrastructure grows, you will probably have more than a single server performing aggregation, especially in the case of multiple datacenter operations.

---

1 There exist several commercial services for RUM, such as Catchpoint, Keynote, Soasta, and ThousandEyes.

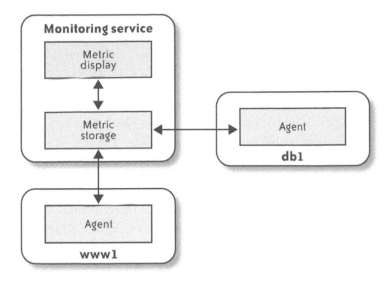

Figure 3-2. *The fundamental pieces of most metric collection systems*

The agent's job is to periodically collect data from the machine on which it's running and send a summary to the metric aggregation server. The metric aggregation server stores the metrics for each of the machines that it's monitoring, which then can be displayed by various methods. Most aggregation servers use some sort of database; one specialized format known as *Round-Robin Database* (RRD) is particularly popular. Other databases used for storing time–series of metrics include OpenTSDB, DalmatinerDB, InfluxDB, Riak TS, BoltDB, and KairosDB. Broadly speaking, the time–series databases use either files or a Log-Structured-Merge Tree (LSM Tree) backed or a B-Tree ordered key/value store.

There exist several daemons to collect metrics. collectd (*https://collectd.org/*) is one of the most common daemons used to collect system and application performance metrics periodically. It has mechanisms to store the values in a variety of ways; for example, RRD files (*http://oss.oetiker.ch/rrdtool/*). collectd supports plug-ins for a large set of applications.

Round-Robin Database and RRDTool

RRDTool is a commonly used utility for storing system and network data—be it a LAMP (Linux, Apache, MySQL, PHP)/MAMP (Mac, Apache, MySQL, PHP) or the modern MEAN (MongoDB, Express.js, Angular.js, Node.js) stack, or even if you are using any other framework (for a link to Richard Clayton's blog on the different frameworks, go to "Resources" on page 100). Here, we offer only an overview, but you can find a full description of RRDTool on the "about" page and in the tutorials at *http:// rrdtool.org*.

The key characteristics of system monitoring data is its size: with cloud computing becoming ubiquitous, the footprint of operational data has experienced an explosive growth, and it is expected to grow at an even faster pace. Thus, ironically, you need to do capacity planning specifically for the data you're collecting for capacity planning! The RRDTool utility solves that by making an assumption that you are interested in fine details only for the recent past. As you move backward in the stored data, it's acceptable to lose some of the details. After some maximum time defined by the user (say, a year), you can let data disappear completely. This approach sets a finite limit on how much data you're storing, with the trade-off being the degree of detail as time moves on. Setting up a retention period is crucial to containing the storage costs. Back when we were at Netflix, we had set up aggressive retention policies for operations data that helped save millions of dollars in AWS S3 cost. Even from a contextual standpoint, storing long periods of operations data might not be useful, because use of stale data can potentially misguide decision-making.

You also can use RRDTool to generate graphs from this data and show views on the various time slices for which you have recorded data. It also contains utilities to dump, restore, and manipulate RRD data, which come in handy when you drill down into some of the nitty-gritty details of capacity measurement. The metric collection tools mentioned earlier in "Capacity Tracking Tools" on page 51 are frontends to RRDTool.

Ganglia

The charts in this chapter were generated by Ganglia (*http://ganglia.info*). We had several reasons for choosing this frontend to present examples and illustrate useful monitoring practices. First, Ganglia was the tool used for this type of monitoring when John was at Flickr. We chose it based partly on some general reasons that might make it a good choice for you, as well: it's powerful (offering good support for the criteria we listed at the beginning of the chapter) and popular. But in addition, Ganglia was developed originally as a grid management and measurement mechanism aimed at high-performance computing (HPC) clusters. Ganglia worked well for Flickr's infrastructure because its architecture is similar to HPC environments, in that Flickr's backend was segmented into separate clusters of machines that each play a different role.

The principles in this chapter, however, are valuable regardless of which monitoring tool you use. Fundamentally, Ganglia works similarly to most metric collection and storage tools. Its metric collection agent is called *gmond* and the aggregation server piece is called *gmetad*. The metrics are displayed using a PHP-based web interface.

Simple Network Management Protocol

The Simple Network Management Protocol (SNMP) is a common mechanism for gathering metrics for most networking and server equipment. Think of SNMP as a standardized monitoring and metric collection protocol. Most routers, switches, and servers support it.

SNMP collects and sends more types of metrics than most administrators choose to measure. Because most networking equipment and embedded devices are closed systems, you can't run user-installed applications such as a metric collection agent like *gmond*. However, as SNMP has long been a standard for networking devices, it provides an easy way to extract metrics from those devices without depending on an agent.

Treating Logs as Past Metrics

Logs are a great way to inject metrics into measurement systems, and it underscores one of the criteria for being able to create custom metrics within a monitoring system.

Web servers can log a wealth of information. When you see a spike in resources on a graph, you often can examine the access and error logs to find the exact moment those resources jumped. Thus, logs make root-cause analysis easier. Most databases have options to log queries that exceed a certain amount of time, allowing you to identify and fix those slow-running queries. Almost everything you use—mail servers, load balancers, firewalls—has the ability to generate logs, either directly or via a Unix-style syslog facility.

In recent years, Splunk as emerged as a leading service for collecting and indexing data, regardless of format or source—logs, clickstreams, sensors, stream network traffic, web servers, custom applications, hypervisors, social media, and cloud services. The structure and schema are applied only at search time.

Monitoring as a Tool for Urgent Problem Identification

As the upcoming section "Applications of Monitoring" on page 61 mentions, problem notification is a separate area of expertise from capacity planning, and generally uses different tools. But some emerging problems are too subtle to trigger health checks from tools such as Nagios. However, you can press the tools we cover in this chapter into service to warn of an impending problem. The techniques in this section also can quickly show you the effects of an optimization. For instance, back at Yahoo!, the Machine Learned Ranking (MLR) team had come up with a new algorithm and was testing its efficacy. Although the quality of search results showed material improvements during A/B testing, the CPU overhead was markedly high. At peak load, the overhead would have made Search BCM (Business Continuity Plan) noncompliant (we discuss BCP further later in this chapter). Based on this, the rollout of the algorithm was gated, thereby avoiding any potential issues in production.

Figure 3-3 shows some anomalous behavior discovered through Ganglia. It represents several high-level views of a few clusters.

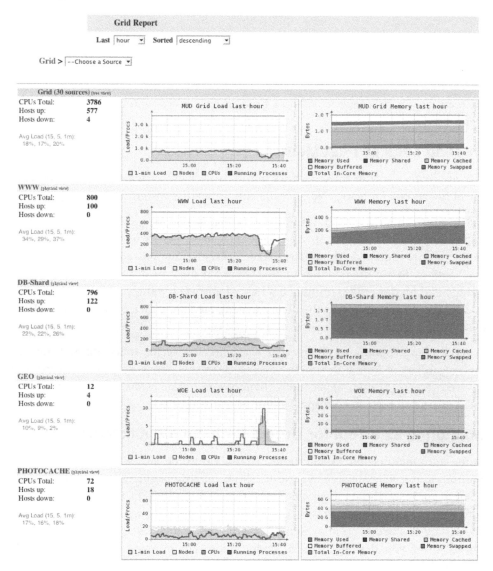

Figure 3-3. *Using metric collection to identify problems*

Without even looking into the details, you can see from the graphs on the left in Figure 3-3 that something unusual has just happened. These graphs cover the load and running processes on the cluster, whereas the groups on the right display combined reports on the memory usage for those clusters. The x-axes for all of the graphs correspond to the same time period, so it's quite easy to see the number of running processes dip in conjunction with the spike in the GEO cluster (notably in the WWW cluster).

The WWW cluster contained Apache frontend machines serving flickr.com, and the GEO cluster was a collection of servers that perform geographic lookups for features such as photo geotagging. By looking at this one web page, you can ascertain where the problem originated (GEO) and where its effects were felt (all other clusters). As it turns out, this particular event occurred when one of the GEO servers stalled on some of its requests. The connections from our web servers accumulated as a result. When the GEO server was restarted, the web servers gradually recovered.

When faults occur with a website, there is tremendous value in being able to quickly gather status information. You would want to be able to get fast answers to the following questions:

- What was the fault?
- When did the fault occur?
- What caused the fault?

In this example, the graphs in Figure 3-3 helped to pinpoint the source of the trouble because you can correlate the event's effects (via the timeline) on each cluster.

Network Measurement and Planning

Capacity planning goes beyond servers and storage to include the network to which they're all connected. The implementation details of routing protocols and switching architectures are beyond the scope of this book, but the network is just like any other resource: finite in capacity and well worth measuring.

NOTE

For references to experience papers from Google, Microsoft, and Facebook on the network topologies and measurement of network latency in their respective datacenters, go to "Readings" on page 98. In addition, the section lists several references to recent research on datacenter networks.

The survey by Chen et al. provides an overview of the features, hardware, and architectures of datacenter networks, including their logical topological connections and physical component categorizations. Recently, tools such as PathDump have been proposed that utilizes resources at edge devices for network debugging.

Networks are commonly viewed as plumbing for servers, and that analogy is apt. When a network is operating well, data simply flows. When it doesn't, everything comes to a grinding halt. This isn't to say that subtle and challenging problems don't crop up with networking: far from it. But for the most part, network devices are designed to do one task well, and their limits should be clear. Network capacity in hosted environments is often a metered and strictly controlled resource; getting data about the usage can be difficult, depending on the contract your organization has with a network provider. As a sanity check of inbound and outbound network usage, aggregate the outward-facing server network metrics and compare them with the bill received from the hosting provider.

When you own your racks and switches, you can make educated decisions about how to divide the hosts across them according to the network capacity they'll need. For example, at Flickr, our photo cache servers demanded quite a bit from their switches, because all they did was handle requests for downloads of photos. We were careful to not put too many of them on one switch so that the servers would have enough bandwidth.

Routers and switches are like servers in that they have various metrics that we can extract (usually with the SNMP protocol) and record. Although their main metrics are the bytes *in* and *out* per second (or packets in and out if the payloads are small), they often expose other metrics, as well, such as CPU usage and current network sessions.

You should measure all of these metrics on a periodic basis with a network graphing tool, such as MRTG or some other utility that can store the history for each metric. Unlike Ganglia and other metric collection tools, MRTG is built with SNMP in mind. Simply because bandwidth usage on the switch and the router is well below the limits of network capacity doesn't mean you're not nearing CPU usage ceilings on those devices—you should monitor all of those metrics with alerting thresholds, as well.

Load Balancing

Load balancers have been a source of much joy and pain in the field of web operations. Their main purpose is to distribute load among pools, or clusters, of machines, and they can range from the simplest to the most complex beasts in a datacenter. Load balancing is usually implemented on the frontend of the architecture, playing traffic cop to web servers that respond to data requests from users' browsers. But load balancers also have been used to spread loads across databases, middle-layer application servers, geographically dispersed datacenters, and mail servers; the list can continue on and on. For example, Amazon EC2 is hosted in multiple locations worldwide. These locations are composed of regions and Availability Zones. Each *region* is a separate geographic area. Each region has multiple, isolated locations known as *Availability Zones*. Elastic Load Balancers (ELBs) automatically distribute incoming application traffic across multiple Amazon EC2 instances.

Load balancers establish load distribution based on a relatively short list of algorithms, which make it possible for you to specify the protocols to balance the traffic across the available servers:

- Round Robin
- Weighted Round Robin
- Weighted Balance
- Priority
- Lowest Latency
- Least Used
- Persistence

> **NOTE**
>
> *Scalable Internet Architectures* by Theo Schlossnagle (Pearson) contains some excellent insights into load balancers and their role in web architectures.

For our purposes, load balancers provide a great framework for capacity management, because they allow the easy expansion and removal of capacity in a production environment. They also offer us a place to experiment safely with various amounts of live web traffic so that you can track the real effect it has on a server's resources. You will see later why this is useful in helping to find a server's ceilings. This can be the joy found with load balancing: convenience in deploying and researching capacity. But there is also pain. Because load balancers are such an integral part of the architecture, failures can be spectacular and dramatic. Not all situations call for load balancing. Even when load balancing is needed, not all balancing algorithms are appropriate.

Jeremy Zawodny recounted a story in the first edition of *High Performance MySQL* (O'Reilly) in which databases at Yahoo! were being load-balanced using a "least connections" scheme. This scheme works quite well when balancing web servers: it ensures that the server with the smallest number of requests has more traffic directed to it. The reason it works with web servers is because web requests are almost always short-lived and on average don't vary to a great extent in size or latency. The paradigm falls apart, however, with databases because not all queries are the same in terms of size and time to process, and the results of those queries can be quite large. The lesson Zawodny leaves us with is just because a database has relatively few current connections does not mean it can tolerate more load.

A second concern with load balancing databases is how to check the health of specific servers within the pool to determine if they all remain capable of receiving traffic. As mentioned earlier, databases are application-specific beasts; hence, what might be suitable for one application might not be suitable for another application. In a similar vein, replication slave lag might be the determining factor for health in one scenario, whereas it could be the current rate of SELECT statements in another scenario. Further complications in load balancing include uncommon protocols, complicated balancing algorithms, and the tuning needed to ensure that load balancing is working optimally for the application.

NOTE

For a reference to Google's software network load balancer, called *Maglev*, go to "Readings" on page 98. Network routers distribute packets evenly to the Maglev machines via Equal-Cost Multipath (ECMP); each Maglev machine then matches the packets to their corresponding services and spreads them evenly to the service endpoints. To accommodate high and ever-increasing traffic, Maglev is specifically optimized for packet processing performance. A single Maglev machine is able to saturate a 10 Gbps link with small packets. Maglev also is equipped with consistent hashing and connection tracking features, to minimize the negative impact of unexpected faults and failures on connection-oriented protocols.

Applications of Monitoring

The remainder of this chapter uses examples to demonstrate some of the important monitoring techniques that you need to know and perform.

Application-Level Measurement

As mentioned earlier, server statistics paint only a part of the capacity picture. You also should measure and record higher-level metrics specific to the application—not specific to one server, but to the entire system. CPU and disk usage on a web server doesn't tell the complete tale of what's happening to each web request, and a stream of web requests can involve multiple pieces of hardware. Example application-level metrics include the number of Tweets/min, number of Photos uploaded/min (Instagram), number of Messages/min (WhatsApp), number of Concurrent Streams/min (Netflix). Further, application-level metrics are often collected at different granularities —by second, by minute, daily, weekly, monthly, or yearly—depending on the use case.

Back at Flickr, application-level metrics were collected on both a daily and cumulative basis. Some of the metrics could be drawn from a database, such as the number of photos uploaded. Others came from aggregating some of the server statistics, such as total disk space consumed across disparate machines. Data collection techniques could be as simple as running a script from a cron job and putting results into its own database for future mining. Some of the metrics tracked included the following:

- Photos uploaded (daily, cumulative)
- Photos uploaded per hour
- Average photo size (daily, cumulative)
- Processing time to segregate photos based on their different sizes (hourly)
- User registrations (daily, cumulative)
- Pro account signups (daily, cumulative)
- Number of photos tagged (daily, cumulative)
- API traffic (API keys in use, requests made per second, per key)
- Number of unique tags (daily, cumulative)
- Number of geotagged photos (daily, cumulative)

Certain financial metrics such as payments received (which are beyond the scope of this book) were also tracked. For any application, it is a good exercise to spend some time correlating business and financial data to the system and application metrics being tracked.

For example, a Total Cost of Ownership (TCO) calculation would be incomplete without some indication of how much these system and application metrics cost the business. Imagine being able to correlate the real costs to serve a single web page of an application. Having these calculations not only would put the architecture into a different context from web operations (business metrics instead of availability, or performance metrics), but they also could provide context for the more finance-obsessed, nontechnical upper management who might have access to these tools.

We can't overemphasize the value inherent to identifying and tracking application metrics. The efforts will be rewarded by imbuing the system statistics with context beyond server health, and will help guide the forecasts. During the procurement process, TCO calculations will prove to be invaluable, as we'll see later.

Now that we've covered the basics of capacity measurement, let's take a look at which measurements you, as the manager of a potentially fast-growing website, would likely want to pay special attention. We discuss the common elements of web infrastructure and list considerations for measuring their capacity and establishing their upper limits. We also provide some examples taken from Flickr's own capacity planning to add greater relevance. The examples are designed to illustrate useful metrics that you might want to track, as well. They are not intended to suggest Flickr's architecture or implementation will fit every application's environment.

Storage Capacity

The topic of data storage is vast. For our purposes, we're going to focus only on the segments of storage that directly influence capacity planning for a high-data-volume website.

One of the most effective storage analogies is that of a glass of water. The analogy combines a finite limit (the size of the glass) with a variable (the amount of water that can be put into and taken out of the glass at any given time). This helps one to visualize the two major factors to consider when choosing where and how to store the data:

- The maximum capacity of the storage media
- The rate at which the data can be accessed

Traditionally, most web operations have been concerned with the first consideration—the size of the glass. However, most commercial storage vendors have aligned their product families with both considerations in mind. In most cases, there are two options in the case of hard disk drives (HDDs):

- Large, slow, inexpensive disks—usually using ATA/SATA protocols

- Smaller, fast, expensive disks—SCSI (Serial Computer System Interface) and SAS (Serial Attached SCSI)

As of January 8, 2017, the price of a Seagate 4TB HDD, 7200 RPM, 6 Gbps, 128 MB cache was $169 and $180 for the SATA and SAS version, respectively. Note that the random or transactional (IOPS) performance of HDDS is dominated by the access time, which in turn is determined by rotational latency and seek time. Interface performance has almost no impact on IOPS. Additionally, interface speed has no measurable effect on sustained performance. The following metrics are typically used to compare the performance of different HDDs:

- Sustained transfer rate

- Average latency

- Operating power

- Idle power

- Cache buffer—size and type

- Mean Time Between Failures (MTBF)

Choosing the "right" HDD always boils down to capacity, performance, and power consumption metrics, but not always in that order. For instance, bulk data and archival workloads require pedestrian performance but copious capacity. Power consumption and capacity are often the key focus in these segments, and performance falls into a distant third place.

Even though the field of data storage has matured, there are still many emerging—and possibly disruptive—technologies of which you should be aware. The popularity of solid-state drives (SSDs)—these are approximately six times more expensive than their HDD counterparts; however, they have a much faster file copy/write speeds than HDDs—and the hierarchical storage schemes that incorporate them might soon become the norm as the costs of storage continue to drop (as illustrated in Figure 3-4) and the raw I/O speed of storage has remained flat in recent years. For transactional workloads, an all-SSD storage solution is likely to have lower overall capital and operational cost than one made from 15,000 RPM HDDs due to the reduction in total slots required to achieve a given transaction performance. Additionally, SSDs have a greatly reduced power footprint compared to spinning drives for a given number of transactions.

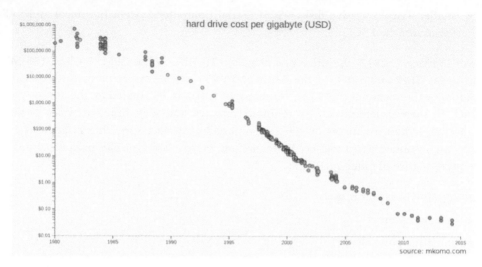

Figure 3-4. *Trend of hard drive cost per gigabyte*

> ── NOTE ────────────────────────────────────
>
> For references to papers describing the anatomy of HDDs (in particular, see Chapter 37 in the book *Operating Systems: Three Easy Pieces*, by R. Arpaci-Dusseau and A. Arpaci-Dusseau), SSDs, and how to characterize their performance, go to "Readings" on page 98.

You can use tools such as Hard Disk Sentinel (*http://hdsentinel.com*) for benchmarking and monitoring of both HDDs and SSDs. Benchmarks such as IOBench and ATTO Disk Benchmark (*http://atto.com/disk-benchmark*) often are used to measure storage performance.

Consumption rates

When planning the storage needs for an application, the first and foremost consideration should be the *consumption rate*. This is the growth in data volume measured against a specific length of time. For sites that consume, process, and store rich media files such as images, video, and audio, keeping an eye on storage consumption rates can be critical to the business. But consumption is important to watch even if storage doesn't grow much at all.

Disk space is about the easiest capacity metric to understand. Even the least technically inclined computer user understands what it means to run out of disk space. For storage consumption, the central question is, "When will I run out of disk space?"

A real-world example: tracking storage consumption

Back at Flickr, a lot of disk space was consumed as photos were uploaded and stored. We'll use this simple case as an example of planning for storage consumption.

When photos were uploaded, they were divided into different groups based on size and then sent to a storage appliance. (Today, most of the media such as images and videos are stored on either private or public clouds that use commodity servers.) A wide range of metrics related to this process were collected:

- How much time it takes to process each image into its various sizes
- How many photos were uploaded?
- The average size of the photos
- How much disk space is consumed by those photos?

Later, we'll see why the aforementioned metrics were chosen for measurement, but for the moment our focus is on the last item: the total disk space consumption over time. This metric was collected and stored on a daily basis. The daily time slice had enough detail to show weekly, monthly, seasonal, and holiday trends. Thus, we could use it to predict when more storage hardware needed to be ordered. Table 3-1 presents disk space consumption (for photos only) for a two-week period.

Table 3-1. *Sample statistics on daily disk space consumption*

Date	Total usage (GB)	Daily usage (GB)
07/26	14321.83	138.00
07/27	14452.60	130.77
07/28	14586.54	133.93
07/29	14700.89	114.35
07/30	14845.72	144.82
07/31	15063.99	218.27
08/01	15250.21	186.21
08/02	15403.82	153.61
08/03	15558.81	154.99
08/04	15702.35	143.53
08/05	15835.76	133.41
08/06	15986.55	150.79
08/07	16189.27	202.72
08/08	16367.88	178.60

The data in Table 3-1 was derived from a cron job that ran a script to record the output from the standard Unix df command on the storage appliances. The data then was aggregated and included on a metrics dashboard. (Data was also collected in much smaller increments [minutes] using Ganglia, but this is not relevant to the current example.) Upon plotting the data from Table 3-1, two observations become clear, as shown in Figure 3-5.

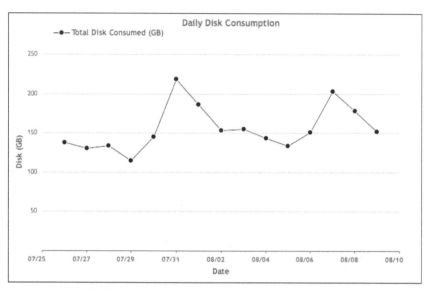

Figure 3-5. *Table of daily disk consumption*

From Figure 3-5, we note that the dates 7/31 and 8/07 were high upload periods. In fact, those dates were both Sundays. Indeed, metrics gathered over a long period revealed that Sundays have always been the weekly peak for uploads. Another general trend that you can see in the chart is that Fridays are the lowest upload days of the week. We'll discuss trends in the next chapter, but for now, it's enough to know that you should be collecting data with an appropriate resolution to illuminate trends. Some sites show variations on an hourly basis (such as visits to news or weather information); others use monthly slices (retail sites with high-volume periods prior to Christmas).

Today, you can use low-cost services such as Amazon's Glacier (*https://aws.amazon.com/glacier/*), Google's Nearline or Coldline Storage (*https://cloud.google.com/storage/archival/*), or Microsoft's Azure's Cool Blob Storage (*http://bit.ly/azure-cool-blob*) for storing long-term data. In the context of operations, a capacity planner should challenge the very retention of long-term data. It is not uncommon to come across cases wherein operations data such as 99th percentile of latency is stored spanning several months or even over a year. Barring events such as a Super Bowl, Christmas, or the like, this is perhaps unwarranted. As discussed earlier in the chapter, setting up retention policies is a common way to contain storage costs of monitoring data.

Storage I/O patterns

How you are going to access storage is the next most important consideration. Is one a video site requiring a considerable amount of sequential disk access? Is one using storage for a database that needs to search for fragmented bits of data stored on drives in a random fashion?

Disk utilization metrics can vary depending on what sort of storage architecture you're trying to measure, but here are the basics:

- How much is the read volume?
- How much is the write volume?
- How long is the CPU waiting for either reading or writing to finish?

Disk drives are the slowest devices in a server. Depending on a server's load characteristic, these metrics could be what defines the capacity for an entire server platform. We can measure disk utilization and throughput a number of ways. The Read/Write performance—transfer rate in Mbps and average/max latency—of an HDD is evaluated along the following dimensions:

- Sequential access
- Random access
- Bursty load

Appendix C lists a lot of useful disk measurement tools.

Whether you're using RAID on a local disk subsystem, a Network-Attached Storage (NAS) appliance, a Storage-Area Network (SAN), or any of the various clustered storage solutions, the metrics that you should monitor remain the same: disk consumption and disk I/O consumption. Tracking available disk space and the rate at which you are able to access that space is irrelevant to which hardware solution you end up choosing; you still need to track them both.

Logs and backup: the metacapacity issue

Backups and logs can consume large amounts of storage, and instituting requirements for them can be a large undertaking. Both backups and logs are part of a typical Business Continuity Plan (BCP) and Disaster Recovery (DR) procedure, so you would need to factor in those requirements along with the core business requirements. Everyone needs a backup plan, but for how long do you maintain backup data? A week? A month? Forever? The answers to those questions will differ from site to site, application to application, and business to business.

For example, when archiving financial information, your organization might be under legal obligation to store data for a specific period of time to comply with regulations. On the other hand, some sites—particularly search engines—typically *maintain* their stored data (such as search logs) for shorter durations in an effort to preserve user privacy.

Storage for backups and log archiving entails identifying how much of each you must have readily available (outlined in retention/purge policies) versus how much you can archive to cheaper (usually slower) hardware. There's nothing particularly special about planning for this type of storage, but it's quite often overlooked because sites don't usually depend on logging and backups for critical guarantees of uptime. We discuss how you should go about measuring the growing storage needs later in this chapter. In Chapter 4, we explore the process of forecasting those needs.

Measuring load on web servers

Web server capacity is application-specific. Generally speaking, web servers are considered frontend machines that accept users' requests, make calls to backend resources (such as databases or other downstream [micro]services), and then use the results of those calls to generate responses. Some applications make simple and fast database queries; others make fewer but more complex queries. Some websites serve mostly static pages, whereas others prepare mainly dynamic content. We will use both system and application-level metrics to take a long view of the usage metrics, which will serve as the foundation for the capacity plan.

Capacity planning for web servers (static or dynamic) is peak-driven and therefore elastic, unlike storage consumption. The servers consume a wide range of hardware resources over a daily period, and have a breaking point somewhere near the saturation of those resources. The goal is to discover the periodic peaks and use them to drive the capacity trajectory. As with any peak-driven resource, you would want to find out when the peaks occur and then explore what's actually going on during those cycles.

A real-world example: web server measurement

As an example, let's take a look at the hourly, daily, and weekly metrics of a single Apache web server. Figure 3-6 presents graphs of all three time frames, from which we'll try to isolate peak periods. The hourly graph reveals no particular pattern, whereas the daily graph shows a smooth decline and rise. Most interesting in terms of capacity planning is the weekly graph, which indicates Mondays undergo the highest web server traffic. As the saying goes: X marks the spot, so let's start digging.

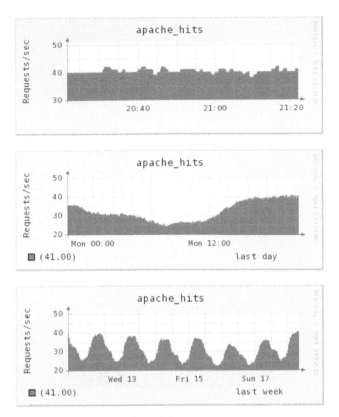

Figure 3-6. *Hourly, daily, and weekly view of Apache requests*

First, let's narrow down what hardware resources we're using. We can pare down this list further by ignoring resources that are operating well within their limits during peak time. Looking at memory, disk I/O, and network resources (not covered in this chapter), we can see none of them come close to approaching their limits during peak times. By eliminating those resources from the list of potential bottlenecks, we already know something significant about the web server capacity. What's left is CPU time, which we can assume is the critical resource. Figure 3-7 displays two graphs tracking CPU usage.

Figure 3-7 demonstrates that at peak, with user and system CPU usage combined, we're just a bit above 50 percent of total CPU capacity. Let's compare the trend with the actual work that is done by the web server so that we can see whether the peak CPU usage has any visible effects on the application layer. Figure 3-8 shows the number of busy Apache processes at each unit of time we measure.

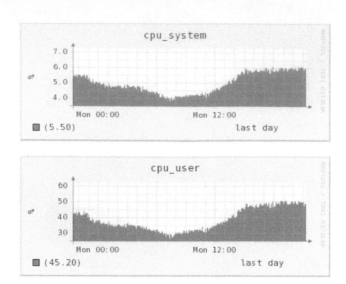

Figure 3-7. *User and system CPU on a web server: daily view*

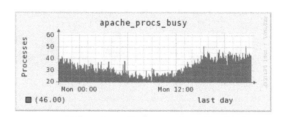

Figure 3-8. *Busy Apache processes: daily view*

The graphs in Figures 3-7 and 3-8 confirm what we might expect: the number of busy Apache processes proportionally follows the CPU usage. Drilling into the most recent RRD values, at 50.7 percent of total CPU usage (45.20 user + 5.50 system), there are 46 Apache processes that are busy. If we were to assume that this relationship between CPU and busy Apache processes stays the same—that is, it's linear—until CPU usage reaches some high (and probably unsafe) value that is not observed in the graphs, you can have some reasonable confidence that the CPU capacity is adequate.

But, hey, that's quite an assumption. Let's try to confirm it through another form of capacity planning: *controlled load testing*.

Finding web server ceilings in a load-balancing environment

You can simplify capturing the upper limit of a web server's resources by a design decision that you have probably already made: using a load balancer. To confirm the ceiling estimates with live traffic, increase the production load—by "pulling" servers (e.g., dialing the weights in HAProxy) from the live pool of servers, which increases the load on the remaining servers commensurately—carefully on some web servers and measure the effects it has on resources. We want to emphasize *the importance of using real traffic instead of running a simulation or attempting to model a web server's resources in a benchmark-like setting.*

The artificially load-balanced exercise confirms the assumption we made in the previous section, which is: the relationship between CPU usage and busy Apache processes remain (roughly) constant. Figure 3-9 graphs the increase in active Apache processes and corresponding CPU usage. This graph was generated from the RRDs produced by one of the web servers throughout its daily peaks and valleys, sorted by increasing amount of total CPU. It confirms CPU usage does indeed follow the number of busy Apache processes, at least between the values of 40 and 90 percent of CPU.

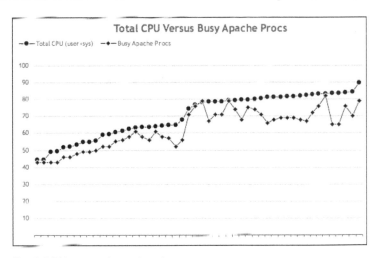

Figure 3-9. *Total CPU versus busy Apache processes*

This suggests that, in the current context, it is safe to use CPU as the single defining metric for capacity on the web servers. In addition, it directly correlates to the work done by the web server—and hopefully correlates further to the website's traffic. Based on this, you can set the upper limit on total CPU to be 85 percent, which gives enough headroom to handle occasional spikes while still making efficient use of the servers.

A little more digging shows the ratio of CPU usage to busy Apache processes to be about 1:1, which allows us to compute one from the other. In general, finding a relationship between system resource statistics and application-level work will be valuable (but is typically not straightforward) when you move on to forecasting usage.

Another benefit of determining the upper limit of a server's resources is that it serves as a key input to check cluster underutilization, thereby boosting operational efficiency. Cluster underutilization has become increasingly common. We can ascribe this to a multitude of reasons; here are just two:

- Lack of knowledge of the upper limit of a server's resources.

- Ease of horizontal scaling on clouds has, in part, shadowed the emphasis on performance optimization. In particular, it is not uncommon to see large instances—be it with respect to compute, memory, or network—on Amazon Web Services (AWS) EC2 being used unnecessarily and clusters being over-provisioned. Tables 3-2 and 3-3 demonstrates that as of January 2017, the prices vary significantly across different instance types on AWS EC2 and Google Compute Engine.

Table 3-2. *Pricing table for AWS*

Effective Hourly

	Reserved[a]	On-Demand
m4.large	$0.062	$0.10
m4.xlarge	$0.124	$0.20
m4.2xlarge	$0.248	$0.40
m4.4xlarge	$0.496	$0.80
m4.10xlarge	$1.239	$2.00
m4.16xlarge	$1.982	$3.20
...		
x1.16xlarge	$4.110	$6.669
x1.32xlarge	$8.219	$13.338

[a] Standard 1-year term with no upfront cost

Table 3-3. *Pricing table for Google Compute*

	Hourly Price
n1-standard-1	$0.05
n1-standard-2	$0.10
n1-standard-4	$0.19
n1-standard-8	$0.38
n1-standard-16	$0.76
n1-standard-32	$1.52
n1-standard-64	$3.04
n1-highmem-2	$0.12
n1-highmem-4	$0.24
n1-highmem-8	$0.47
n1-highmem-16	$0.95
n1-highmem-32	$1.89
n1-highmem-64	$3.79
n1-highcpu-2	$0.07
n1-highcpu-4	$0.14
n1-highcpu-8	$0.28
n1-highcpu-16	$0.57
n1-highcpu-32	$1.13
n1-highcpu-64	$2.27

Arun (along with his colleagues) had addressed the aforementioned issues back at Netflix, which reduced the operational footprint by several million dollars.

Owing to this, the burn rate increases and then, as an afterthought, operational efficiency comes to the forefront.

Production Load Testing with a Single Machine

When you have the luxury of using a load balancer to add and remove servers to and from production, it makes the task of finding capacity ceilings easy. But when you have only a single machine, things become somewhat more difficult. How can you increase load on that one machine?

You certainly can't call the users and ask them to start clicking faster, but you can add load on a server by *replaying* requests that you have seen in production. Many tools are available to do this:

- Httperf (*http://www.hpl.hp.com/research/linux/httperf/*)
- JMeter (*http://jmeter.apache.org*)
- Iago (*https://github.com/twitter/iago*)
- The Grinder (*http://grinder.sourceforge.net/*)
- Tsung (*http://tsung.erlang-projects.org/*)
- Taurus (*http://gettaurus.org/*)
- Siege (*http://www.joedog.org/siege-home/*)

For an extensive discussion of the various performance testing tools, go to *http://www.opensourcetesting.org/category/performance/*. Most of these tools allow you to replay requests (which are essentially HTTP URLs) at varying speeds against a server. This makes it possible for you to increase load very slowly and carefully, which is critical in a single-machine environment—you should not do any load testing that would kill the only running server. You should use this not-very-safe technique only to stretch the server's abilities a little at a time under safe conditions such as during a low-traffic period.

Artificial load testing, even by replaying real production logs, brings with it a whole slew of limitations. Even though these tools give fine-grained control over the rate of requests, and you can control what requests are being made, they still don't accurately portray how the server will behave under duress. For example, depending on how you allow the application to change data, simulating production loads with logs of previous requests can be difficult. You might not want to rewrite data that you have already written, so you would need to do some massaging of the logs being replayed.

Another limitation is common to all web load-testing scenarios: an accurate representation of the client/server relationship. By using Httperf or Siege, you can simulate multiple clients, but in reality, all of the requests will be coming from a single client node that's running the script. A workaround for running these tools from a single machine is to run the scripts from multiple machines. A tool called Autobench (*http://www.xenoclast.org/autobench/*) is a Perl wrapper around Httperf that enables Httperf to be run from multiple hosts in a coordinated fashion. Autobench can also aggregate the results.

Even Autobench produces different results from real-world requests. Clients can be all over the globe, with wildly different network latencies, connection speeds, and many other variables. Also, you need to be careful about cranking up the request rate from a single client machine. You might run out of client resources before you run out of server resources, which will further taint the results. Be sure to stay within the client's file descriptor maximums, network limits, and CPU limits during these artificial tests.

Instead of spending time working around the limitations of artificial load testing, you should consider upgrading the architecture to make it easier to find a server's upper limits. A load balancer—even with just one extra server—not only helps to find the limits, but provides a more robust architecture overall.

Database Capacity

Nearly every dynamic website uses some form of a database to keep track of its data. This means that you need to provide the capacity for it. In the good old days of the LAMP/MAMP world, MySQL and Postgres used to be the favorite databases, whereas Oracle, Microsoft SQL Server, and myriad others also serve as the backend data store for many successful sites.

Outside of the basic server statistics, there are a number of database-specific metrics you would want to track:

- Queries-per-second (SELECTs, INSERTs, UPDATEs, and DELETEs)
- Connections currently open
- Lag time between master and slave during replication
- Cache hit rates

Planning the capacity needs of databases—particularly clusters of them—can be tricky business. Establishing the performance ceilings of databases can be difficult because there might be hidden cliffs that only reveal themselves in certain edge cases.

For example, back at Flickr, it was assumed that the databases running on a given hardware platform had a ceiling of X queries-per-second before performance began to degrade unacceptably. It was surprising to learn that some queries performed fine for a user with fewer than 10,000 photos, but slowed down alarmingly for a user who had more than 100,000 photos. So, ceilings for the database server that handled users with large numbers of photos were redefined. This type of creative sleuthing of capacity and performance is mandatory with databases and underscores the importance of understanding how the databases are actually being used outside the perspective of system statistics.

At this stage, we'll reiterate our point about performance tuning. As pointed out in Jeremy Zawodny and Derek Balling's book, *High Performance MySQL*, database performance often depends more on the schemas and queries than on the speed of the hardware. Because of this, developers and database administrators focus on optimizing their schemas and queries, knowing that doing so can change the performance of the database quite dramatically. This in turn, affects the database ceilings. One day you might think that you need 10 database servers to get 20,000 queries-per-second; the next day you might find that you need only five. This is because the developers were able to optimize some of the more common (or computationally expensive) queries.

A real-world example: database measurement

Databases are complex beasts, and finding the limits of a database can be time-consuming but well worth the effort. Just as with web servers, database capacity tends to be peak-driven, meaning that their limits are usually defined by how they perform during the heaviest periods of end-user activity. As a result, we generally take a close look at the peak traffic times to see what's going on with system resources, and then take it from there.

But before we begin hunting for the magical "red line" of database consumption, remember, it is recommended to look at how a database performs with *real* queries and *real* data. One of the first things to determine is when the database is expected to run out of hardware resources relative to traffic. Depending on the load characteristics, you might be bound by the CPU, the network, or disk I/O.

If you're lucky enough to keep the most-requested data in memory, you might find CPU or network resources to be the constraints. This situation makes the hunt for a performance ceiling a bit easier because you would need to track only a single number, as it was discovered when monitoring Apache performance. If data is substantially larger than what you can fit into physical memory, the database's performance will be limited by the slowest piece of equipment: the physical disk. Because of the random nature of database-driven websites, queries for data on databases tend to be yet even more random, and the resulting disk I/O is correspondingly random. Random disk I/O tends to be slow, because the data being requested is bound by the disk's ability to seek back and forth to random points on the platter. Therefore, many growing websites eventually have disk I/O as their defining metric for database capacity. Depending on whether a website or mobile app is read-heavy (for example, the *New York Times* (*http://nytimes.com/*)) versus write-heavy (such as Facebook (*http://facebook.com/*) or Instagram) as well as the SLA, the selection of the type of underlying storage—be it HDD or SSD—should be made accordingly (refer to the section "Storage Capacity" on page 62).

Let's use one of the servers as an example. Figure 3-10 shows the relevant MySQL metrics for a single user database during a peak hour. It depicts the rate of concurrent MySQL connections along with the rate of INSERTs, UPDATEs, DELETEs, and SELECTs per second for a single hour. There are a few spikes during this time in each of the metrics, but only one stands out as a potential item of interest.

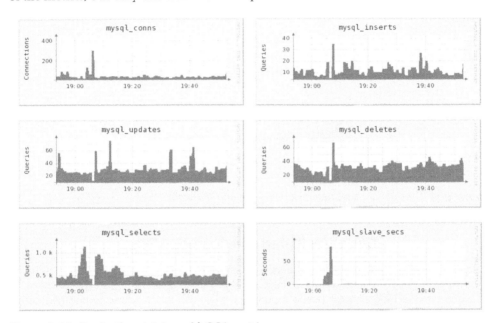

Figure 3-10. *Production database MySQL metrics*

The bottom graph shows the amount of database replication lag experienced during the last hour; it peaks at more than 80 seconds. Presence of lag of this degree in database replication generally means that the slaves temporarily lack a lot of the recent data loaded onto the master. If all user queries are directed to the slaves, which means until the slaves catch up to the master, users won't see the most up-to-date data. This can cause various unwelcome effects, such as a user annotating a photo, clicking the Submit button, but not seeing that comment right away. This is confusing for the user and can result in all sorts of out-of-sync weirdness. Even if you were to know from past experience that the databases are disk I/O bound, you would still want to confirm that by taking a look at disk utilization and I/O wait in Figure 3-11.

In this example, Ganglia was used to collect and plot disk utilization statistics for the database. These are reported every 60 seconds by some of the fields returned by the Linux *iostat* command, %iowait and %ioutil. Note on the graph that although disk utilization jumped up to 100 percent more than once, it was only during the period when I/O wait exceeded the 40 percent mark that the MySQL replication lag jumped.

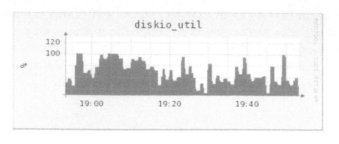

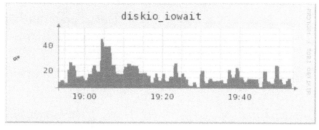

Figure 3-11. *Production database disk utilization and I/O wait*

Curiosity Killed the Capacity Plan

Let's take a moment to address a question that might have arisen in your mind: if the spike is not specific to a hardware defect, and is indeed due to a legitimate database event, what is triggering it? This is a pertinent question, but its answer won't get you any further in assessing how many database servers will be needed to handle the traffic.

There will always be spikes in resource usage, bugs, bad queries, and other unforeseen hiccups. The job as a capacity planner is to take the bad with the good and assume that the bad won't go away. Of course, after one has submitted hardware purchase justifications, by all means, don your performance-tuning hat and go after the cause of that spike with a vengeance. Indeed, finding the cause should be a mandatory next step, just don't let the investigation of one anomaly get in the way of forecasting capacity needs.

What does this mean? With nothing more than a cursory look at the metrics, we can deduce that replication slave lag is caused by disk I/O wait rather than disk utilization. We can further deduce that the replication lag becomes a problem only at a disk I/O wait of 40 percent or higher. Keep in mind that these results apply only to a particular configuration; this is an example rather than a general rule. The results make us wonder: could they indicate something defective with this particular server? Possibly, and the hypothesis should be easy enough to verify by provoking the behavior on similar production hardware. In this case, the examination of graphs from other servers demonstrates the relationship to be a general one that applied to Flickr activity at the time: other databases of identical hardware in production experience replication lag starting in, or near 40 percent disk I/O wait.

Armed with these metrics, it can be said with high confidence that the 40 percent disk I/O wait threshold is the ceiling for this database. As it relates to hardware configuration and the database query mix and rate, you should plan on staying below 40 percent disk I/O wait. But what does that mean in terms of actual database work? Before we dig into the numbers a bit further, let's apply the same test method as we did with the web servers: increase production load on the database.

Finding database ceilings

A more focused and aggressive approach to finding database ceilings is to slowly (but again, carefully) increase the load on a live production server. If you maintain only a single database, this can be difficult to do safely. With only a single point of failure, testing runs the risk of bringing the site down entirely. This exercise becomes markedly easier if your organization employs any sort of database load balancing (via hardware appliance or within the application layer). Figure 3-12 revisits the diagram of a common database architecture, this time with more real-world details added.

In this scenario, all database write operations are directed to the master; read functions are performed by database slaves. The slaves are kept up-to-date by replication. To pinpoint the ceilings of the database slaves, you want to increase the load on one of them by instructing an application to favor that particular device. If your organization operates a hardware load balancer for the databases, you might be able to weight one of the servers higher than the others in the balanced pool.

Increasing load to a database in this manner can reveal the effects load has on the resources, and hopefully expose the point at which the load will begin to affect replication lag. In our case, we'd hope to confirm the educated guess of 40 percent disk I/O wait is the upper limit that the database can withstand without inducing replication lag.

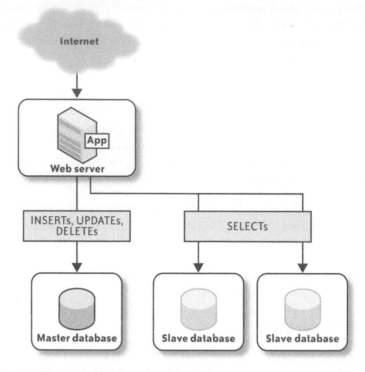

Figure 3-12. *A master-slave database architecture*

This example reflects a common database capacity issue defined by disk I/O. The databases might be CPU-, memory-, or network-bound, but the process of finding the ceiling of each server is the same.

Caching Systems

We mentioned earlier that disks are the slowest pieces of an infrastructure, which makes accessing them expensive in terms of time. Most large-scale sites alleviate the need for making these expensive operations by caching data in various locations.

In web architectures, caches are most often used to store database results (as with Memcached) or actual files (as with Squid or Varnish). Both approaches call for the same considerations with respect to capacity planning. They are examples of *reverse proxies,* which are specialized systems that cache data sent from the web server to the client (usually a web browser).

First, let's take a look at the diagram in Figure 3-13 to see how Squid and Varnish caching normally works with servers. As Figure 3-14 shows, the diagram differs only slightly when illustrating database caching in the style of Memcached.

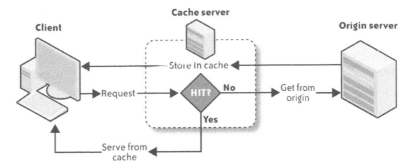

Figure 3-13. *Basic content server caching mechanisms (reverse-proxy)*

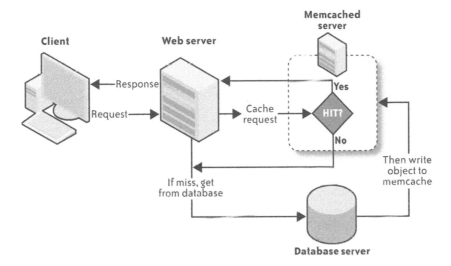

Figure 3-14. *Database caching*

Cache efficiency: working sets and dynamic data

The two main factors affecting cache capacity are the size of the *working set*—the amount of memory that a process (*https://en.wikipedia.org/wiki/Process_(computing)*) requires in a given time interval—and the extent to which the data is dynamic or changing.

How often the data changes will dictate whether you would choose to cache that data. On one end of the spectrum is data that almost never changes. Examples of this type of data include usernames and account information. On the other end of the spectrum is information that changes frequently, such as the last comment made by a user, or the last photo uploaded. Figure 3-15 illustrates the relationship between caching efficiency and types of data.

It should be obvious that there's no benefit in caching data that changes frequently, because the proxy will spend more time invalidating the cache than retrieving data from it. Every application will have its own unique characteristics with respect to caching, so there isn't any rule of thumb to follow. However, measuring and recording the cache's hit ratio is imperative to understanding how efficient it is. This can help guide your capacity plan and hopefully steer how (and when) you would want to cache objects.

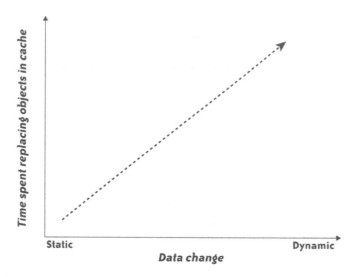

Figure 3-15. *Cache efficiency depends on rate of change*

The other major consideration is the size of the working set of cacheable objects. Caches have a fixed size. The working set of cacheable objects is the number of unique objects, whether database results or files, that are requested over a given time period. Ideally, you would have enough cache capacity to handle the entire working set. This would mean the vast majority of requests to the cache would result in cache hits. However, in real terms, there could be many reasons why you can't keep all the objects you want in cache. You would then need to depend on something called *cache eviction* to make room for new objects coming in. We'll present more on cache eviction later.

To function, caching software needs to keep track of its own metrics internally. Because of this, most caches expose those metrics, allowing them to be measured and recorded by the monitoring tools. Back at Flickr, we used Squid for reverse-proxy caching of photos. Slower, cheaper, and larger-capacity disks were used to store the photos. At the same time, caching systems that use smaller and faster disks to serve those photos were also employed. The number of caching servers was horizontally scaled as the request rate for photos increased. Additionally, the backend persistent storage was horizontally scaled as the number of photos grew. Each caching server had a limited amount of disk and memory available to use as cache. Because the working set of photos was too large to fit into the caches, the caches used to fill up. A full cache needs to constantly make decisions on which objects to evict to make room for new objects coming in. This process is based on a replacement or "eviction" algorithm. There are many eviction algorithms, but one of the most common is *Least Recently Used* (LRU), which is demonstrated in Figure 3-16.

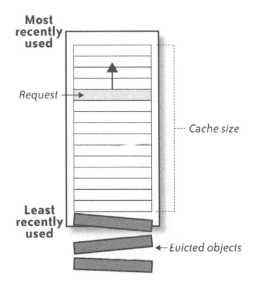

Figure 3-16. *The LRU cache eviction algorithm*

Here are some other popular cache eviction algorithms:

- First In First Out (FIFO)
- Last In First Out (LIFO)
- Least Frequently Used (LFU)

───── **NOTE** ──────────────────────────────────

For a reference to a survey by Podlipnig and Boszormenyi, go to "Readings" on page 98.

───

As requests come into a cache, the objects are organized into a list based on when each was last requested. A cache-missed object, once retrieved from the origin server, will be placed at the top of the list, and a cache hit will also be moved from its current location to the top of the list. This keeps all of the objects in order from most recently used to least recently used. When the cache needs to make room for new objects, it will remove objects from the bottom of the list. The age of the oldest object on the list is known as the *LRU reference age*; this is an indicator of how efficient the cache is, along with the hit ratio.

The LRU algorithm is used in Memcached, Squid, Varnish, and countless other caching applications. Its behavior is well known and relatively simple to understand. Squid offers a choice of some more complex eviction algorithms, but nearly all of the most popular database caches use the LRU method. Following are the most important metrics to track with any caching software:

- Cache hit ratio
- Total request rate
- Average object size
- LRU reference age (when using the LRU method)

Let's take a look at some caching metrics (compiled using Squid) from production.

Establishing Caching System Ceilings

The capacity of caching systems is defined differently depending on their usage. For a cache that can hold its entire working set, the request rate and response time might dictate its upper limits. In this case, you again can make use of the same method that was applied to web serving and database disk I/O wait: carefully increase the load on a server in production, gather metric data along the way, and tie system resource metrics (CPU, disk I/O, network, memory usage) to the caching system metrics listed in the previous section.

Determining the ceiling of a cache when it is constantly full and must continually evict objects is a complicated exercise. It might better be defined not by request rate, but by its hit ratio (and indirectly, its reference age).

Table 3-4 summarizes cache planning considerations.

Table 3-4. *Cache planning considerations*

Type of cache use	Characteristics	Cache ceilings	Resource ceilings
Small or slowly increasing working set	100 percent contained in cache	Request rate	Disk I/O utilization and wait, CPU and memory usage
Large or growing working set	Moving window, constant eviction (churn)	Hit ratio, LRU reference age	Cache size

A real-world example: cache measurement

As we mentioned earlier, at Flickr all of the metrics mentioned in the previous section were considered. The caches were constantly full, and cache eviction is a continuous process as users regularly upload new photos. Squid's memory and disk cache were measured, as well. Let's first take a look at the graphs in Figure 3-17 to see what effect request rates had on the system resources.

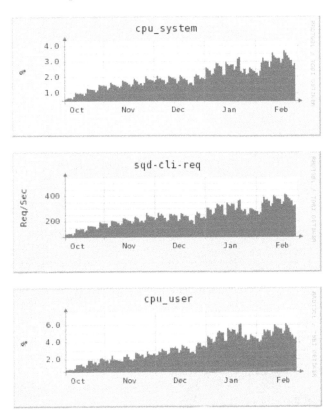

Figure 3-17. *Five-month view of Squid request rate and CPU load (user and system)*

As you can see from the graphs, the Squid request rate increased steadily within the time period shown. The zigzag pattern represents the weekly peak activity periods (Mondays). For the same time period, the total CPU usage has increased, as well, but there was no immediate risk of running out of CPU resources. Because there was an extensive use of disk cache on the Squid servers, you would want to take a look the disk I/O usage, as well; refer to Figure 3-18 for the results. The figure confirms what was suspected: the amount of operations waiting for disk activity follows the rate of requests in near perfect synchronization. Because one now knows that the Squid server uses the disk more than any other resource, such as CPU or memory, this tells us that the defining peak resource metric is disk I/O wait—the same as the database ceiling. If you were to zoom into the data using RRDTool to overlay disk I/O wait and request rate, you could plot them against each other in Excel, as shown in Figure 3-19.

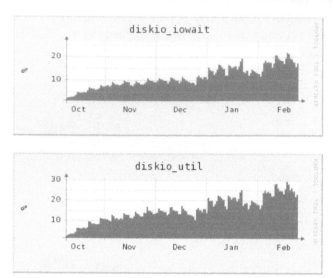

Figure 3-18. *Five-month view of Squid server disk I/O wait and utilization*

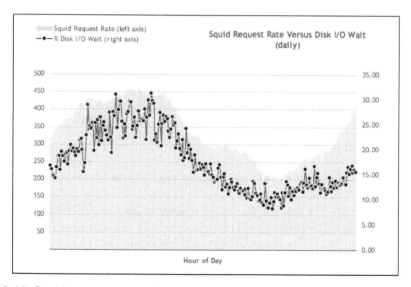

Figure 3-19. *Squid request rate versus disk I/O wait: daily view*

Now that the correlation has been established, let's sort the data in Excel as a function of increasing order and plot it again. As illustrated in Figure 3-20, this permits us to more easily see the trends related to the amount of the data requested at a particular moment. Now, we can clearly see how the two metrics relate to each other as they go up and how disk I/O wait affects Squid's performance.

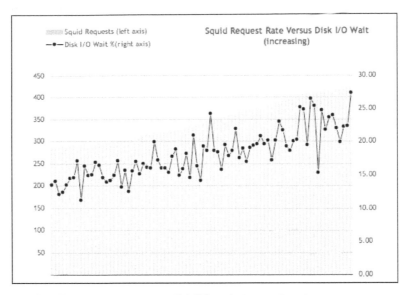

Figure 3-20. *Squid request rate versus disk I/O wait: increasing view*

Squid keeps internal metrics regarding the time it takes to handle both cache hits and misses. One can collect those metrics in Ganglia, as well. We're not very concerned about the time spent for cache misses, because for the most part that doesn't inform us as to the upper limits of the cache—handling a miss mostly strains the network and origin server. Hits come from Squid's memory and disk cache, so that merits attention. Figure 3-21 presents the results over a five-month period.

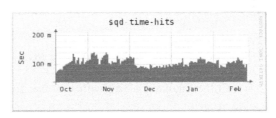

Figure 3-21. *Squid hit time (in milliseconds): five-month view*

This illustrates how the time for a cache hit has not changed significantly over the time period we're measuring (hovering around 100 milliseconds). Note that Squid's "time-to-serve" metrics include the time until the client finishes receiving the last byte of the response, which can vary depending on how far the clients are from the server. This informs us that although disk I/O wait has increased, it has not affected the response time of the Squid server—at least not with the load it has been experiencing. We'd like to keep the time-to-serve metric within a reasonable range so that the user isn't forced to wait for photos, so we've arbitrarily set a maximum time-to-serve of 180 milliseconds for this particular server; we'll still want to stay below that. But what amount of traffic *will* push the time-to-serve above that threshold?

To find out, let's go to the stalwart load-increasing exercise—increase production load slowly on the servers while recording their metrics. Based on the context, you should watch for the following: the threshold at which disk I/O wait begins to affect cache hit response time. You should increase the request rate to the Squid server slowly to avoid completely flooding the hit ratio. As depicted in Figure 3-22, by either replaying URLs via Httperf or Siege, or by removing servers from a load-balanced pool, the request rate can be bumped up gradually on a single Squid server.

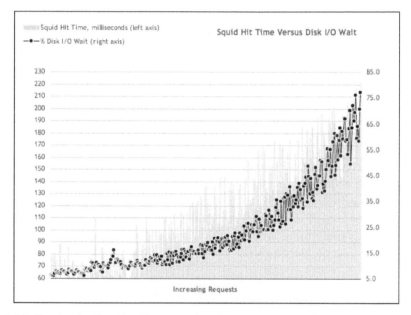

Figure 3-22. *Testing for Squid ceilings: serving time versus disk I/O wait*

As you can see, the service time increases along with the disk I/O wait time (no surprise there). Due to a wide range of photo sizes, there's a lot of variation in the data for time-to-serve, but you would note serving times of 180 milliseconds at approximately 40 percent disk I/O wait. The only task remaining is to find the request rate at which that threshold was hit (see Figure 3-23). Here, the "red line" can be seen—at 40 percent disk I/O wait, upward of 850 requests per second can be processed. If time-to-serve were to be used as a guide, this is going to be the maximum performance that you can expect from the hardware platform with this particular configuration.

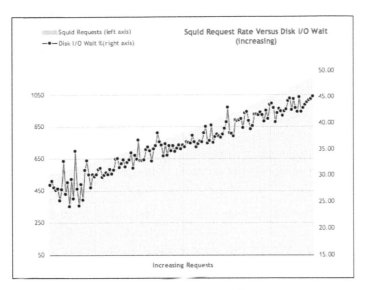

Figure 3-23. *Squid request rate versus disk I/O wait, ceiling*

However, we're not done with the cache measurements. You also should analyze how the cache's efficiency—with respect to hit ratio and LRU reference age—changes over time owing to a dynamic working set. Figure 3-24 presents the results from a five-month view.

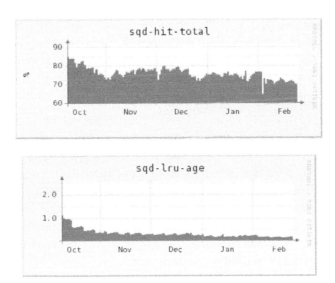

Figure 3-24. *Cache hit ratios (percent) and LRU age (days): five-month view*

These two graphs display the hit ratio and LRU reference age of a particular Squid caching server that was used to serve images over a period of five months. The hit ratio is expressed as a percentage, and the LRU reference age as units of days. During that time, LRU age and hit rate have both declined at a small but discernible rate, which we can attribute to the increase in photos being uploaded by users. As the working set of requested photos grows, the cache needs to work increasingly harder to evict objects to make room for new ones. But even with this decrease in efficiency, it appears that with a 72 percent hit rate, the LRU reference age for this server is about three hours. This is nothing to sneeze at and is acceptable in the current context. You would want to keep an eye on the hit rate as time goes on and continue to tune the cache size as appropriate.

To summarize, this exercise involved two metrics related to the ceilings experienced by the caching system: disk I/O wait and cache efficiency. As the request rate goes up, so does the demand on the disk subsystem and the time-to-serve. At roughly 850 requests per second, what was deemed to be an acceptable end-user experience could be maintained. In general, as you approach the SLA, the number of cache servers should be increased so as to comfortably handle the load. The ceiling of 850 requests per second assumed a steady cache hit ratio (which in practice can also change over time).

Special Use and Multiple Use Servers

In the web server example, CPU usage was the defining metric. Admittedly, this makes the job pretty easy; we have a fixed amount of CPU to work with. It was also made less difficult by virtue of the fact that Apache was the only significant application using the CPU. There are many circumstances, though, in which we don't have the luxury of dedicating each server to do a single task. Having a server perform more than one task—email, web, uploads—can make more efficient use of the hardware, but it complicates taking measurements.

The approach thus far has been to tie system resources (CPU, memory, network, disk, and so on) to application-level metrics (Apache hits, database queries, etc.). When you run many different processes, it's difficult to track how their usage relates to one another, and how each process might signal that it's reaching the upper limits of efficient operation. Further, in a cloud environment, there might be processes of others running on the same node/cluster; that is, the environment might be multitenant, which is very typical of public clouds. But simply because this scenario can complicate capacity measurements, you need not assume that it makes planning impossible.

To discern what processes are consuming which resources, you'll want to do one of the following:

- Isolate each running application or microservice and measure its resource consumption.
- Hold some of the applications' resource usage constant in order to measure one at a time.

The process requires some poking around in the data to find situations in which events just happen to run controlled experiments implicitly. For instance, as we'll see in the example later in this section, it was noticed that two days had similar web server traffic but different CPU usage. This oddity could have been exploited potentially to find out the constraints on capacity for the web server.

Back at Flickr, the photo upload and processing tasks resided on the same machines that were serving pages for the Flickr.com website; that configuration made capacity planning difficult. Image processing is a CPU-intensive task, and as the number of uploads increased, so did the dependence on disk I/O resources. Add to that the increase in traffic, and it was discovered that three different jobs were all fighting for the same resources.

At any given moment, it wasn't exactly certain how much hardware was being used for each process, so the following application-level metrics were additionally measured to guide the estimates:

- Photo uploads (which mostly drove disk I/O and network utilization)
- Image processing (which drove CPU utilization)
- Serving the site's pages (which drove both memory and CPU utilization)

Based on prior knowledge of the traffic pattern and shape for each system metric, the latter could be correlated to the tasks they were doing. The objective was to isolate the resource effects of each of those tasks to track them separately, or at least get a good idea of what was doing what. Having these metrics already stored in RRD files, their values were dumped to text and then loaded into Excel for graphing and analysis.

First, a two-day period was found in which the pattern of web traffic was similar for both days (Figure 3-25). At that time, the burden on the web servers included not only serving the site's page, but taking in photo uploads and processing them, as well.

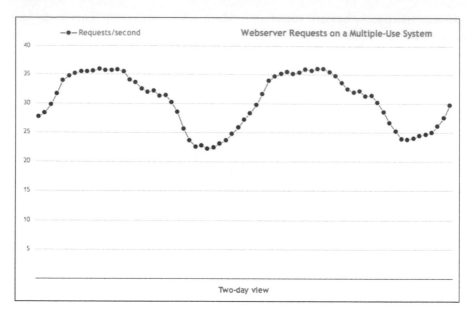

Figure 3-25. *Two-day view of Apache requests*

Now let's take a look at the system resources. In Figure 3-26, the CPU usage from Figure 3-25 is overlaid onto the web server data for the same time period.

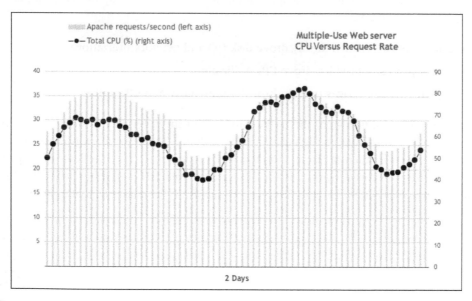

Figure 3-26. *Web server work versus total CPU: two-day view*

Clearly, the CPU was working harder on the second day, even though the amount of Apache traffic was roughly the same. The only other task this server was doing was image processing; so, we could attribute the different CPU usage to image processing. Figure 3-27 uncovers what was suspected: the extra CPU consumption on the second day was due to photo processing. This activity actually occurred over a weekend, and, as mentioned earlier in the chapter, Sundays are a high upload day. Figure 3-28 plots the photo processing rates for both days against each other and shows the differences. Note that while the peaks for Sunday were more than 20 percent higher, during the evening the rate dropped below that of Saturday's rates at the same time, making the difference negative on the graph.

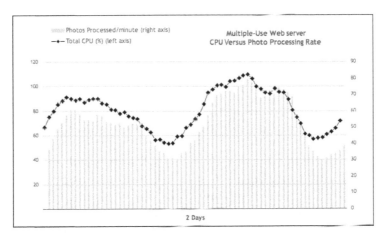

Figure 3-27. *Total CPU versus photo processing rate, two-day view*

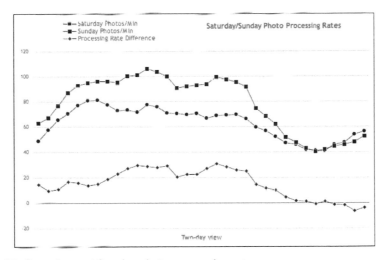

Figure 3-28. *Saturday and Sunday photo processing rates*

Figure 3-29 highlights that, at least for the weekend under consideration, every 30 photos processed per minute corresponds to an additional 25 percent CPU utilization.

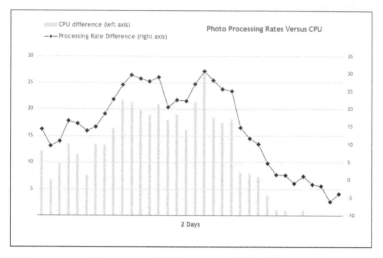

Figure 3-29. *Photo processing rate and CPU usage, distilled from two-day data*

This is an extremely rough estimate based on a small sample, and you should consider this nothing more than an example of how to isolate resource usage on a multiple-use system. Confirming this 25:30 ratio using proper rigor would mean looking at a larger range of traffic and upload rates and comparing the data again. But this process gives us a starting point from which the ceilings can be determined. In this situation, an ideal scenario is one in which the two variables (web traffic and upload rates) are being tracked and we can figure out how many machines are needed if both processes run on each machine. This process worked for more than a year in planning the capacity for Flickr's web servers. Eventually, image processing was assigned its own dedicated cluster that could take advantage of multicore CPUs—another example of diagonal scaling at work.

API Usage and Its Effect on Capacity

As more and more websites use open APIs to provide access to their services to external developers, capacity planning for the use of those services must follow. You might have guessed by now that we are strong advocates of application-level metrics as well as system metrics and API usage is the area where application-level metrics can matter the most. When you allow others access to data via an open API, you are essentially allowing a much more focused and routine use of a website.

One of the advantages of having an open API is that it allows for more efficient use of an application. If external developers wanted to gain access to data and no API methods existed, they might *screen scrape* the site's pages to get at the data, which is extremely inefficient for a number of reasons. If they're interested only in a specific piece of data on the page, they'd still need to request the entire page and everything that entails, such as downloading CSS markup, JavaScript, and other components necessary for a client's browser to render the page, but is of no interest to the developer. Although APIs allow more efficient use of an application, if not tracked properly, they also expose a web service to potential abuse because they enable other applications to ask for those specific pieces of data. To address this, it is has become routine for services that expose an API—such as Google Maps and Facebook Graph API—to rate-limit the call rate on a per-endpoint basis. Even consumer-facing services such as Google Search have set up checks to curtail traffic driven by bots.

Having some way to measure and record the usage of an open API on a per-user, or per-request-method basis, should be considered mandatory in capacity tracking on a site offering a web API. This is commonly done through the use of unique API *keys* or other unique credentials. Upon each call to the API, the key identifies the application and the developer responsible for building the application. Because it's much easier to issue an enormous volume of calls to an API than to use a regular client browser, you should keep track of what API calls are being made by what application, and at what rate.

Back at Flickr, any key that appeared to be abusing the API was automatically invalidated, according to provisions outlined in the Terms of Service. A running total was maintained every hour for a) every API key that made a call, b) how many calls were made, and c) the details of each call (refer to Figure 3-30 for the basic idea of API call metrics). With this information, you can identify which API keys are responsible for the most traffic—you can potentially set up a tiered pricing system based on this. You should keep track of the details of each key, as shown in Figure 3-31.

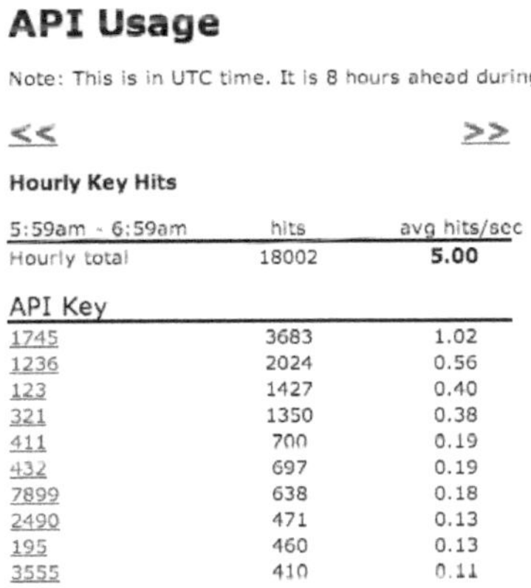

API Usage

Note: This is in UTC time. It is 8 hours ahead during daylight savings.

<<   >>

Hourly Key Hits

5:59am - 6:59am	hits	avg hits/sec
Hourly total	18002	**5.00**

API Key		
1745	3683	1.02
1236	2024	0.56
123	1427	0.40
321	1350	0.38
411	700	0.19
432	697	0.19
7899	638	0.18
2490	471	0.13
195	460	0.13
3555	410	0.11

Figure 3-30. *Keeping track of API request statistics*

API Key #623

Last hour:	6,816 queries - 0.95 qps
Last day:	76,782 queries - 0.85 qps
Last month:	94,239 queries - 0.84 qps

ID:	623
API Key:	12356ef1323fa3213x
Developer Name:	John Bacon
Developer Email:	piggy@bacon.com
Developer Account:	ilovepork (all keys)
Applying Notes:	I want to display Flickr photos on my website.

Commercial Key:	No

Auth'd User Count:	13 (View list)
Auth Secret:	cade1234f1235
Auth Title:	BaconViewer
Auth Description:	Allow BaconViewer to read your private photos.
Auth URL:	http://bacon.com/baconviewer/
Auth Mode:	Web (Callback: None)

Issue Date:	10 Mar	3.48AM PDT
Expiry Date:	12 Apr	3.48AM PDT

Unique methods: 10

flickr.photos.getInfo	812 hit(s)
flickr.photos.search	794 hit(s)
flickr.photosets.getInfo	653 hit(s)
flickr.photosets.getContext	415 hit(s)
flickr.photosets.getPhotos	274 hit(s)

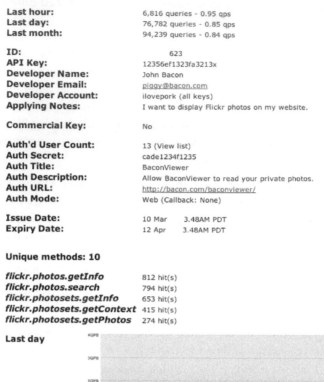

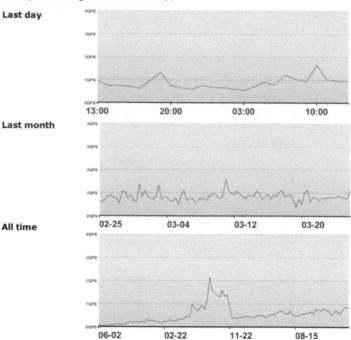

Figure 3-31. *API key details and history*

By collecting this information on a regular basis, you will have a much better idea of how API usage affects the resource consumption. You then can adjust API limits as the capacity landscape changes.

Examples and Reality

Each application and type of data affects system resources differently. The examples in this chapter simply illustrate the methods and thought processes by which you can investigate and form a better understanding of how increased load can affect each part of an infrastructure. The important lesson to retain is that each component of an architecture will spend system resources to serve the website, and you should ensure that the consumption of those resources is measured accurately. However, recording the right measurements isn't enough. You need to have some idea of when those resources will run out, and that's why you should periodically reestablish those ceilings. This is particularly important in the context of Agile development for which the performance profile of a given application or microservice can change materially in a short amount of time.

Running through the exercise of finding the upper limits of an architecture can reveal the bottlenecks that you didn't even know existed. As a result, you might make changes to the application, hardware, network, or any other component responsible for the problem. Every time you make a change to the architecture, you should check the resource ceilings again, because they're likely to change. This shouldn't be a surprise, because capacity planning is a process, not a one-time event.

Summary

Measurement is a necessity, not an option. It should be viewed as the eyes and ears of an infrastructure. It can inform all parts of an organization: finance, customer care, engineering, and product management.

Capacity planning can't exist without the measurement and history of a system and application-level metrics. Planning is also ineffective without knowing a system's upper performance boundaries so that you can avoid approaching them. Finding the ceilings of each part of an architecture involves the same process:

1. Measure and record the server's primary function.

   Examples: Apache hits, database queries

2. Measure and record the server's fundamental hardware resources.

   Examples: CPU, memory, disk, network usage

3. Determine how the server's primary function relates to its hardware resources.

   Example: n database queries result in m percent CPU usage

4. Find the maximum acceptable resource usage (or ceiling) based on both the server's primary function and hardware resources by using one of the following methods:

   - Artificially (and carefully) increasing real production load on the server through manipulated load balancing or application techniques.

   - Simulating as close as possible a real-world production load.

Readings

Performance

1. J. M. Anderson et al. (1997). *Continuous profiling: where have all the cycles gone?*

2. G. Ren et al. (2010). *Google-Wide Profiling: A Continuous Profiling Infrastructure for Data Centers.*

3. J. Dai et al. (2011). *HiTune: dataflow-based performance analysis for big data cloud.*

4. M. Kambadur et al. (2012). *Measuring interference between live datacenter applications.*

5. Ú. Erlingsson et al. (2012). *Fay: Extensible Distributed Tracing from Kernels to Clusters.*

6. B. Gregg. (2012). *Thinking Methodically about Performance.*

7. M. Schwarzkopf et al. (2013). *Omega: flexible, scalable schedulers for large compute clusters.*

8. C. Wang et al. (2013). *Performance troubleshooting in data centers: an annotated bibliography?*

9. S. Mahlke et al. (2013). *Instrumentation sampling for profiling datacenter applications.*

10. A. Verma et al. (2015). *Large-scale cluster management at Google with Borg.*

11. S. Kanev et al. (2015). *Profiling a warehouse-scale computer.*

12. B. Burns et al. (2016). *Borg, Omega, and Kubernetes: Lessons learned from three container-management systems over a decade.*

13. W. Hassanein. (2016). *Understanding and improving JVM GC work stealing at the data center scale.*

14. Y. Zhang et al. (2016). *History-based harvesting of spare cycles and storage in large-scale datacenters.*

Network

1. A. Singh et al. (2015). *Jupiter Rising: A Decade of Clos Topologies and Centralized Control in Google's Datacenter.*

2. C. Guo et al. (2015). *Pingmesh: A Large-Scale System for Data Center Network Latency Measurement and Analysis.*

3. Y. E. Sung et al. (2016). *Robotron: Top-down Network Management at Facebook Scale.*

4. R. Govindan et al. (2016). *Evolve or Die: High-Availability Design Principles Drawn from Googles Network Infrastructure.*

5. P. Tammana et al. (2016). *Simplifying datacenter network debugging with PathDump.*

6. Y. Geng et al. (2016). *Juggler: a practical reordering resilient network stack for datacenters.*

7. K. He et al. (2016). *AC/DC TCP: Virtual Congestion Control Enforcement for Datacenter Networks.*

8. T. Chen, X. Gao and G. Chen. (2016). *The features, hardware, and architectures of data center networks.*

9. W. M. Mellette et al. (2016). *P-FatTree: A multi-channel datacenter network topology.*

Load Balancer

1. D. E. Eisenbud et al. (2016). *Maglev: a fast and reliable software network load balancer.*

Storage

1. C. Ruemmler and J. Wilkes. (1993). *UNIX Disk Access Patterns.*

2. C. Ruemmler and J. Wilkes. (1994). *An introduction to disk drive modeling.*

3. D. Anderson et al. (2003). *More Than an Interface—SCSI vs. ATA.*

4. D. Anderson. (2003). *You Don't Know Jack About Disks.*

5. W. W. Hsu and A. J. Smith. (2004). *The performance impact of I/O optimizations and disk improvements.*

6. J. Elerath. (2007). *Hard Disk Drives, The Good, Bad and Ugly.*

7. M. K. McKusick. (2012). *Disks from the Perspective of a File System: Disks lie. And the controllers that run them are partners in crime.*

8. M. Cornwell. (2012). *Anatomy of a Solid-state Drive.*

Database and Caching

1. P. J. Denning. (1968). *The working set model for program behavior.*

2. P. J. Denning. (1980). *Working Sets Past and Present.*

3. H.-T. Chou and D. J. DeWitt. (1985). *An Evaluation of Buffer Management Strategies for Relational Database Systems.*

4. E. J. O'Neil et al. (1993). *The LRU-K Page Replacement Algorithm for Database Disk Buffering.*

5. R. Nishtala et al. (2013). *Scaling Memcache at Facebook.*

6. S. Podlipnig and L. Boszormenyi. (2003). *A Survey of Web Cache Replacement Strategies.*

Resources

1. "A Working Theory-of-Monitoring." (2013) *https://www.usenix.org/conference/lisa13/working-theory-monitoring.*

2. "eBPF and systems performance." (2017) *https://www.oreilly.com/ideas/ebpf-and-systems-performance.*

3. "Runtime metrics." *https://docs.docker.com/engine/admin/runmetrics.*

4. "Linux Performance Analysis in 60,000 Milliseconds." (2015) *http://www.brendangregg.com/Articles/Netflix_Linux_Perf_Analysis_60s.pdf.*

5. "Linux Performance." *http://www.brendangregg.com/linuxperf.html.*

6. "UNIX Load Average Part 1: How It Works." (2010) *http://www.teamquest.com/files/9214/2049/9761/ldavg1.pdf.*

7. "UNIX Load Average Part 2: Not Your Average Average." (2010) *http://www.teamquest.com/import/pdfs/whitepaper/ldavg2.pdf.*

8. "Understanding load averages and stretch factors." (2007) *http://www.linux-magazine.com/content/download/62593/485442/Load_Average.pdf.*

9. "Systemtap tutorial." (2015) *https://sourceware.org/systemtap/tutorial.pdf*.

10. "ktap GitHub repo." *https://github.com/ktap/ktap*.

11. "Thoughts on Time-series Databases." (2015) *http://jmoiron.net/blog/thoughts-on-timeseries-databases*.

12. "MEAN's great, but then you grow up." (2014) *https://rclayton.silvrback.com/means-great-but-then-you-grow-up*.

13. "Load Balancing Methods & Algorithms." *http://www.peplink.com/technology/load-balancing-algorithms/*.

14. "SSD vs HDD." *http://www.storagereview.com/ssd_vs_hdd*.

15. "The sorry state of server utilization and the impending post-hypervisor era." (2013) *http://bit.ly/sorry-state-server*.

16. "How one startup hopes to solve server underutilization." (2015) *http://bit.ly/solve-server-under*.

17. "Cache replacement policies—References." *http://bit.ly/cache-replacement-policies*.

## CHAPTER FOUR

Predicting Trends

We assume that you have made a few passes through Chapter 3 and have just deployed a monitoring, trending, graphing, and measurement system. Now you can use this data (excluding the barking statistics) like a crystal ball and predict the future like Nostradamus. But, let's stop here for a moment to remember an irritating little detail: *it's impossible to accurately predict the future.*

Forecasting capacity needs is part context and part math. It's also the art of slicing and dicing of historical data and making educated guesses about the future. Outside of those rare bursts and spikes of load on the system, the long-term view is hopefully one of steadily increasing usage. By putting all of this historical data into perspective, you can generate estimates for what your organization would need to sustain the growth of a website. As we'll see later, the key to making robust forecasts is to have an *adjusta ble* process. In the cloud context, the forecasts guide the design of the autoscaling policies (the topic of autoscaling is discussed in detail in Chapter 6).

(When to) Buy or Lease

The topic of whether to buy or lease has been researched for more than five decades in a wide variety of fields such as real estate, automobiles, and, of course, cloud computing. (For references to prior research work on the topic go to the section "Readings" on page 134.) Before you become too excited about charting massive growth and putting new servers in place to handle the deluge, you need to remind yourself of one of the key economic factors to be dealt with: buying hardware—be it on the cloud or in an on-premises datacenter—too early is wasteful.

This rule is rooted in the obvious trend in computing costs: all forms of hardware are becoming cheaper, even as they become faster and more reliable. Whether Moore's Law (Gordon E. Moore's now-famous axiom in 1965 that postulates that the number of transistors on an integrated circuit approximately doubles every eighteen months) holds true forever, we can predict that manufacturers will continue to lower costs over time—this is illustrated in Figure 4-1. If your organization can wait six months before buying a piece of equipment, you will likely end up with faster and less-expensive equipment at that time.

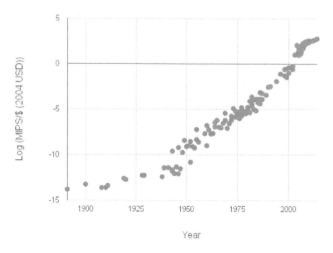

Figure 4-1. Trend of compute per dollar (source: *http://bit.ly/trends-costs*)

Certainly, you don't want to be caught unprepared when growth takes place—this book is all about saving you from that career-threatening situation. Conversely, the company financial officers will not hold you in high regard either when you have purchased a lot of equipment that lies idle, only to see its price drop a few months later.

Riding the Waves

A good capacity plan depends on knowing your enterprise's needs for the most important resources and how those needs change over time. After the historical data on capacity has been gathered, you can begin analyzing it with an eye toward recognizing any trends and recurring patterns. Recall the example from Chapter 3 when we were both working at Flickr, and we discovered that Sunday had been historically the highest photo upload day of the week. This is interesting for many reasons. It also can lead one to other questions: has that Sunday peak changed over time and, if so, how has it changed with respect to the other days of the week? Has the highest upload day always been Sunday? Does that change with addition of new members residing on the other side of the International Date Line? Is Sunday still the highest upload day on holiday weekends? These questions can all be answered when the data is available and the answers in turn can provide a wealth of insight with respect to planning new feature launches, operational outages, or maintenance windows.

Recognizing trends is valuable for many reasons, not just for capacity planning. When we looked at disk space consumption in Chapter 3, we stumbled upon some weekly upload patterns. Being aware of any recurring patterns can be invaluable when making decisions later on. Trends also can inform community management, customer care and support, and product management and finance. Following are some examples of how metrics measurement can be useful:

- An operations group can avoid scheduling maintenance on a Sunday because it could affect machines that are tasked with image processing. Instead, opting to perform maintenance on Friday can potentially minimize any adverse effects on users.

- If new code that touches the upload processing infrastructure is deployed, you might want to pay particular attention the following Sunday to see whether everything is holding up well when the system experiences its highest load.

- Making customer support aware of these peak patterns allows them to gauge the effect of any user feedback regarding uploads.

- Product management might want to launch new features based on the low or high traffic periods of the day. A good practice is to ensure that everyone on the team knows where these metrics are located and what they mean.

- The finance department also might want to know about these trends because it can help it plan for capital expenditure (capex) costs.

Trends, Curves, and Time

Let's take a look back at the daily storage consumption data from Chapter 3 and forecast the future storage needs. We already know the defining metric: total available disk space. Graphing the cumulative total of this data provides the right perspective from which to predict future needs. Taking a look at Figure 4-2, we can see where consumption is headed, how it's changing over time, and when storage is likely to be exhausted.

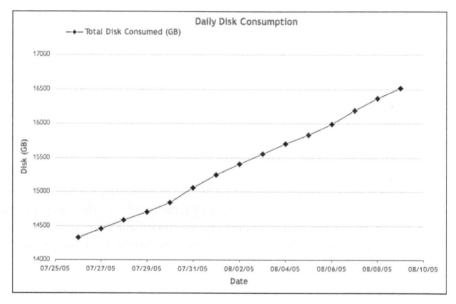

Figure 4-2. *Total disk consumption: cumulative view*

Now, let's add another constraint: the total currently available disk space. Let's assume for this example that there's a total of 20 TB (or 20,480 GB) installed capacity. From the graph, we note that about 16 TB of storage has been consumed. Adding a solid line extending into the future to represent the total installed space, we obtain the graph shown in Figure 4-3. This illustration demonstrates a fundamental principle of capacity planning: predictions require two essential bits of information—the ceilings and the historical data.

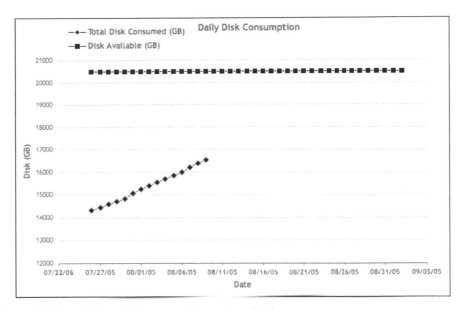

Figure 4-3. *Cumulative disk consumption and available space*

Determining when the space limitation would be reached is the next step. As just suggested, we could simply draw a straight line that extends from our measured data to the point at which it intersects the current limit line. But is the growth actually linear? It might not be.

Excel calls this next step "adding a trend line," but some readers might know this process as *curve fitting*. This is the process by which you attempt to find a mathematical equation that mimics the data at hand. You then can use that equation to make educated guesses about missing values within the data. In this case, because the data is on a timeline, the missing values of interest are in the future. Finding a good equation to fit the data can be just as much art as science. Fortunately, Excel is one of many programs that offers curve fitting.

To display the trend using a more mathematical appearance, let's change the Chart Type in Excel from Line to XY (Scatter). XY (Scatter) changes the date values to just single data points. We then can use the trending feature of Excel to show us how this trend looks at some point in the future. Right-click the data on the graph to open a drop-down menu. On that menu, select Add Trendline. A dialog box opens, as shown in Figure 4-4.

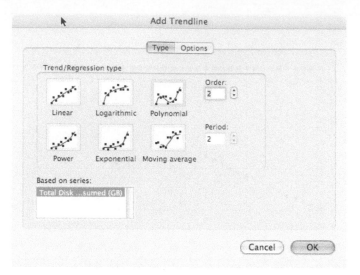

Figure 4-4. *Add Trendline Type dialog box*

Next, select a trend line type. For the time being, let's choose Polynomial, and set Order to 2. There might be good reasons to choose another trend type, depending on how variable the data is, how much data you have, and how far into the future you want to forecast. (For more information, see the upcoming sidebar, "Fitting Curves")

In this example, the data appears about as linear. However, based on domain knowledge, we already know that this data isn't linear over a longer period of time (it's accelerating). Therefore, let's pick a trend type that can capture the acceleration.

After selecting a trend type, click the Options tab, which opens the Add Trendline Options dialog box, as shown in Figure 4-5. To show the equation that will be used to mimic disk usage, select the checkbox for "Display equation on chart." You also can look at the R^2 value for this equation by selecting the "Display R-squared value on chart" checkbox. The R^2 value is known in the world of statistics as the *coefficient of determination*. Without going into the details of how this is calculated, it's basically an indicator of how well an equation matches a certain set of data. An R^2 value of 1 indicates a mathematically perfect fit. With the data we're using for this example, any value above 0.85 should be sufficient. The important thing to know is that as the R^2 value decreases, so too should the confidence in the forecasts. Changing the trend type in the previous step affects the R^2 values—sometimes for better, sometimes for worse —so some experimentation is needed here when looking at different sets of data.

Add Trendline

Type | Options

Trendline name

- ◉ Automatic: Poly. (Total Disk Consumed (GB))
- ○ Custom: [|]

Forecast

Forward: [0] ⊕ Units

Backward: [0] ⊕ Units

- ☐ Set intercept = [0]
- ☐ Display equation on chart
- ☐ Display R-squared value on chart

(Cancel) (OK)

Figure 4-5. *The Add Trendline Options dialog box*

Fitting Curves

In capacity planning, curve fitting is where the creative can collide with the scientific. In most cases, capacity planning is used to stay ahead of growth, which is generally represented through time-series data that extends upward and to the right in some form or manner.

Figuring out how and when the data gets there is the challenge, and we aim to use *forecasting* to solve it. Forecasting is the process of constructing new data points beyond a set of known data points. In our case, we're going to be defining new data points that exist in the future of time-series data.

The difficulty with curve fitting and forecasting lies in the reconciliation between what we know about the data source and the apparent best-fit equation. Simply because you find a curve that fits the data with 99.999% mathematical accuracy doesn't mean it's going to be an accurate picture of the future. The data will almost always have context outside of the mathematical equation. For example, forecasting the sale of snow shovels must include considerations for time of year (winter versus summer) or geography (Alaska or Arizona).

When finding equations to fit the data, it's also best to stay away from higher-order models. It can be tempting to use higher-order models because their fit (*coefficient of determination*) is very good, but anything higher than a second-order model often exhibits dramatic fluctuations outside of the dataset at hand. This is commonly referred to as *overfitting* in statistical learning and machine learning parlance. Splines are a commonly used family of curve fitting models. There exists a large body of work on linear and nonlinear curve fitting. For references for prior research work on the topic, go to "Readings" on page 134.

The horizon of forecasting is usually determined on a case-by-case basis. For instance, small startup companies might need only to know how much money it must spend for the next three months. In contrast, public companies need to have an estimate of capex spending for the remainder of the year. In general, subject to the underlying characteristics, the longer the horizon, the lower the accuracy of the forecasts.

The moral of the story is to use a good deal of common sense when curve-fitting data. Don't insist on elegantly perfect fits, because they are quite often the result of questionable assumptions.

You would want to extend the trend line into the future, of course. The trend line should be extended far enough into the future such that it intersects the line corresponding to our total available space. This is the point at which you can predict that the space will run out. In the Forecast portion of the dialog box, type 25 units for a value. Our units in this case are days. After clicking OK, the forecast should look similar to Figure 4-6.

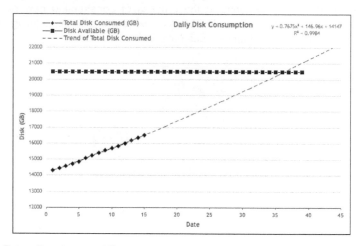

Figure 4-6. *Extending the trend line*

The graph indicates that somewhere around day 37, the disk space will run out. Luckily, you don't need to squint at the graph to see the actual values; you have the equation used to plot that trend line. As detailed in Table 4-1, plugging the equation into Excel, and using the day units for the values of X, the last day when the disk usage is below the disk space limit is 8/30.

Table 4-1. *Determining the precise day when disk space will run out*

	Date	Disk available (GB)	$Y = 0.7675 x2 + 146.96x + 14147$
33	08/27	20480.00	19832.49
34	08/28	20480.00	20030.87
35	08/29	20480.00	20230.79
36	08/30	20480.00	20432.24
37	08/31	20480.00	20635.23
38	09/01	20480.00	20839.75
39	09/02	20480.00	21045.81

Now that it is known when more disk space will be needed, you can get on with ordering and deploying it.

This example of increasing disk space is about as simple as they come. But because the metric is consumption-driven, every day has a new value that contributes to the definition of our curve. You also need to factor in the peak-driven metrics that drive the capacity needs in other parts of a site. Peak-driven metrics involve resources that are continually regenerated, such as CPU time and network bandwidth. They fluctuate more dramatically and thus are more difficult to predict, so curve fitting requires more care.

Tying Application Level Metrics to System Statistics: Database Example

In Chapter 3, we went through an exercise of how to establish database ceiling values. To recap, 40 percent disk I/O wait was a critical value to avoid because at this threshold the database replication began experiencing disruptive lags. How do you know when this threshold will be reached? You need some indication that the ceiling is near. It appears the graphs don't show a clear and smooth line just bumping over the 40 percent threshold. Instead, the disk I/O wait graph shows that the database is healthy until a 40 percent spike occurs. You might deem occasional (and recoverable) spikes to be acceptable, but you need to track how the average values change over time so that the spikes aren't so close to the ceiling. Also, I/O wait times should be tied to database usage, and ultimately, what that means in terms of actual application usage.

To establish some control over this unruly data, let's take a step back from the system statistics and look at the purpose this database is actually serving. In this example, we're looking at a *user* database wherein the data and the metadata of the users is stored: their photos, their tags, the groups they belong to, and more. The two main drivers of load on this database are the number of photos and the number of users. Having said that, neither the number of users nor the number of photos is singularly responsible for how much work the database does. Taking only one of those variables into account means ignoring the effect of the other. Indeed, there might be many users who have few, or no photos; queries for their data would be quite fast and not at all taxing. On the flip side, there might be a handful of users who maintain enormous collections of photos. You can look at the metrics for clues for the critical values.

For the running example, let's find out the single most important metric that can define the ceiling for each database server. To this end, we should analyze the disk I/O wait metric for each database server and determine whether there exists a high correlation between I/O wait and the number of users in the database. Referring back to our days at Flicker, it's interesting to note that there were some servers with more than 450,000 users, but they had healthy levels of I/O wait. On the other hand, other servers with only 300,000 users experienced much higher levels of I/O wait. Looking at the number of photos wasn't helpful either—disk I/O wait didn't appear to be tied to photo population. As it turned out, the metric that directly indicated disk I/O wait was the ratio of *photos-to-users* on each of the databases.

Again, back at Flickr, as part of an application-level dashboard, the metrics—how many users are stored on each database along with the number of photos associated with each user—were measured on a daily basis (collected each night). The photos-per-user ratio is simply the total number of photos divided by the number of users. Although this could be thought of as an average photos-*per*-user, the range can be quite large, with some "power users" having many thousands of photos, whereas a majority have only tens or hundreds. By looking at how the *peak* disk I/O wait changes with respect to this photos-per-user ratio, we can get an idea of what sort of application-level metrics we can use to predict and control capacity utilization (see Figure 4-7).

The graph shown in Figure 4-7 was compiled from a number of databases at Flickr and displays the peak disk I/O wait values against the corresponding current photos-to-user ratios. With this graph, we can ascertain where disk I/O wait begins to jump up. There's an elbow in the data around the 85–90 ratio when the amount of disk I/O wait jumps above the 30 percent range. Because the ceiling value is 40 percent, you would want to keep the photos-per-user ratio in the 80–100 range. We can control this ratio within the application by distributing photos for high-volume users across many databases.

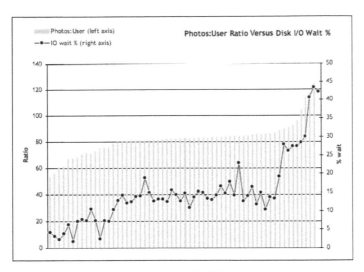

Figure 4-7. *Database—photo:user ratio versus disk I/O wait percent*

At Flickr, after reaching the limits of the more traditional Master/Slaves MySQL replication architecture (in which all writes go to the master and all reads go to the slaves), the database layout was redesigned to be *federated*, or *sharded*. This evolution in architecture exemplifies how architecture decisions can have a positive effect on capacity planning and deployment. By federating the data across many servers, the growth at Flickr was limited only by the amount of hardware that we could deploy, not by the limits imposed by any single machine.

Because we were federated, we could control how users (and their photos) are spread across many databases. This essentially meant that each server (or pair of servers, for redundancy) contained a unique set of data. This is in contrast to the more traditional monolithic database that contains every record on a single server.

NOTE

You can find more information about federated database architectures in Cal Henderson's book *Building Scalable Web Sites* (O'Reilly).

OK, enough diversions—let's get back to the database capacity example and summarize. Database replication lag is bad and should be avoided. Replication lag occurred at 40 percent disk I/O wait, which in turn was reached when the photos-per-user ratio reached 110. Based on the knowledge of how our photo uploads and user registrations grow (see Figure 4-8), we can make informed decisions regarding how much database hardware to buy, and when.

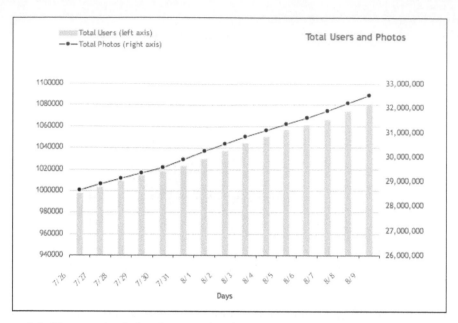

Figure 4-8. *Photos uploaded and user registrations*

We can extrapolate a trend based on this data to predict how many users and photos there will be for the foreseeable future, and then use that to gauge how the photos-per-user ratio will look on our databases, and whether there is a need to adjust the maximum amounts of users and photos to ensure an even balance across those databases.

Forecasting Peak-Driven Resource Usage: Web Server Example

When we forecast the capacity of a peak-driven resource, we need to track how the peaks change over time. From there, we can extrapolate from that data to predict future needs. Our web server example is a good opportunity to illustrate this process. In Chapter 3, we identified our web server ceilings as 85 percent CPU usage for this particular hardware platform. We also confirmed CPU usage is directly correlated to the amount of work Apache is doing to serve web pages. Also, as a result of our work in Chapter 3, we should be familiar with what a typical week looks like across Flickr's entire web server cluster. Figure 4-9 illustrates the peaks and valleys over the course of one week.

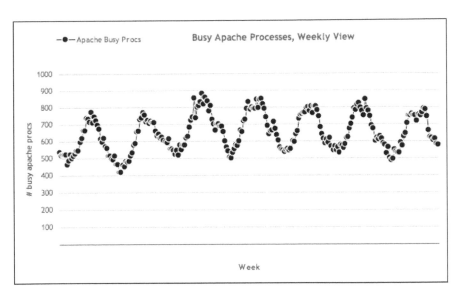

Figure 4-9. *Busy Apache processes: weekly view*

This data is extracted from a time in Flickr's history when it had 15 web servers. Let's suppose that this data is taken today, and we have no idea how our activity will look in the future. We can assume the observations we made in Chapter 3 are accurate with respect to how CPU usage and the number of busy apache processes relate— which turns out to be a simple multiplier: 1.1. If for some reason this assumption *does* change, we'll know quickly because we're tracking these metrics on a per-minute basis. According to the graph in Figure 4-9, we're seeing about 900 busy concurrent Apache processes during peak periods, load balanced across 15 web servers. That works out to about 60 processes per web server. Thus, each web server is using approximately 66 percent total CPU (we can look at our CPU graphs to confirm this assumption).

The peaks for this sample data are what we're interested in the most. Figure 4-10 presents this data over a longer time frame, in which we see these patterns repeat.

It's these weekly peaks that we want to track and use to predict our future needs. As it turns out, for Flickr, those weekly peaks almost always fall on a Monday. If we isolate those peak values and pull a trend line into the future as we did with our previous disk storage example, we'll see something similar to Figure 4-11.

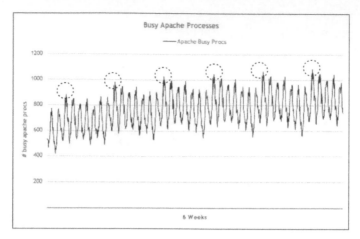

Figure 4-10. *Weekly web server peaks across six weeks*

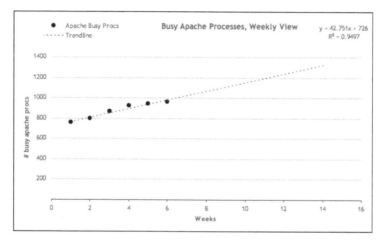

Figure 4-11. *Web server peak trend*

If our traffic continues to increase at the current pace, this graph predicts that in another eight weeks we can expect to experience roughly 1,300 busy Apache processes running at peak. With our 1.1 processes-to-CPU ratio, this translates to around 1,430 percent total CPU usage across our cluster. If we have defined 85 percent on each server as our upper limit, we would need 16.8 servers to handle the load. Of course, manufacturers are reluctant to sell servers in increments of tenths, so we'll round that up to 17 servers. We currently have 15 servers, so we'll need to add two more.

The next question is, when should we add them? As we explained in the earlier sidebar, we can waste a considerable amount of money if we add hardware too soon. Fortunately, we already have enough data to calculate *when* we'll run out of web server capacity. We have 15 servers, each currently operating at 66 percent CPU usage at peak. Our upper limit on web servers is set at 85 percent, which would mean 1,275 percent CPU usage across the cluster. Applying our 1.1 multiplier factor, this in turn would mean 1,160 busy Apache processes at peak. If we trust the trend line shown in Figure 4-12, we can expect to run out of capacity sometime between the 9th and 10th week.

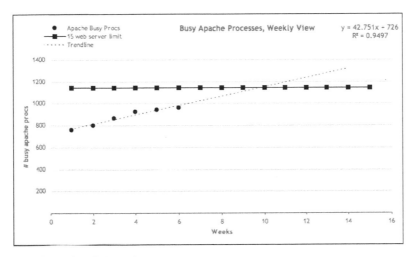

Figure 4-12. *Capacity of 15 web servers*

Therefore, the summary of our forecast can be presented succinctly:

- We'll run out of web server capacity three to four weeks from now.
- We'll need two more web servers to handle the load we expect to see in eight weeks.

Now we can begin our procurement process with detailed justifications based on hardware usage trends, not simply a wild guess. We'll want to ensure that the new servers are in place before we need them, so we'll need to find out how long it will take to purchase, deliver, and install them.

This is a simplified example. Adding two web servers in three to four weeks shouldn't be too difficult or stressful. Ideally, we should have more than six data points for robust forecasting, and you would likely not be so close to a cluster's ceiling as in our example. But no matter how much capacity you would need to add or how long the time frame actually is, the process should be the same.

Caveats Concerning Small Datasets

When you are forecasting with peak values as we've done, it's important to remember that the more data you have to fit a curve, the more accurate the forecast will be. In our example, we based our hardware justifications on six weeks' worth of data. Is that enough data to constitute a trend? Possibly, but the time period on which you are basing the forecasts is of great importance, as well. Maybe there is a seasonal lull or peak in traffic, and you are on the cusp of one. Maybe you are about to launch a new feature that will add extra load to the web servers within the time frame of this forecast. These are only a few considerations for which you might need to compensate when making justifications to buy new hardware. A lot of variables can come into play when predicting the future, and, as a result, we need to remember to treat our forecasts as what they really are: educated guesses that need constant refinement.

Automating the Forecasting

Our use of Excel in the previous examples was pretty straightforward. But you can automate that process by using Excel macros. And because you would most likely be doing the same process repeatedly as the metric collection system churns out new usage data, you can benefit greatly by introducing some automation into this curve-fitting business. Other benefits can include the ability to integrate these forecasts into a dashboard, plug them into other spreadsheets, or put them into a database.

An open source program called *fityk (http://fityk.sourceforge.net/)* does a great job of curve-fitting equations to arbitrary data and can handle the same range of equation types as Excel. For our purposes, the full curve-fitting abilities of fityk are a distinct overkill. It was created for analyzing scientific data that can represent wildly dynamic datasets, not just growing and decaying data. Although fityk is primarily a GUI-based application (see Figure 4-13), a command-line version is also available, called cfityk. This version accepts commands that mimic what would have been done with the GUI, so you can use it to automate the curve fitting and forecasting.

The command file used by cfityk is nothing more than a script of actions that you can write using the GUI version. After you choreograph the procedure in the GUI, you can replay the sequence with different data via the command-line tool.

If you have a carriage return–delimited file of x-y data, you can feed it into a command script that can be processed by cfityk. The syntax of the command file is relatively straightforward, particularly for our simple case. Let's go back to our storage consumption data for an example.

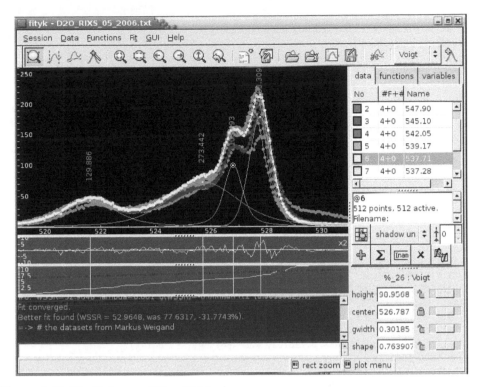

Figure 4-13. *The fityk curve-fitting GUI tool*

In the code example that follows, we have disk consumption data for a 15-day period, presented in increments of one data point per day. This data is in a file called *storage-consumption.xy* and appears as displayed here:

```
 1 14321.83119
 2 14452.60193
 3 14586.54003
 4 14700.89417
 5 14845.72223
 6 15063.99681
 7 15250.21164
 8 15403.82607
 9 15558.81815
10 15702.35007
11 15835.76298
12 15986.55395
13 16189.27423
14 16367.88211
15 16519.57105
```

The cfityk command file containing our sequence of actions to run a fit (generated by using the GUI) is called *fit-storage.fit* and appears as shown here:

```
# Fityk script. Fityk version: 0.8.2
@0 < '/home/jallspaw/storage-consumption.xy'
guess Quadratic
fit
info formula in @0
quit
```

This script imports our x-y data file, sets the equation type to a second-order polynomial (quadratic equation), fits the data, and then returns back information about the fit, such as the formula used. Running the script gives us these results:

```
$cfityk ./fit-storage.fit
1> # Fityk script. Fityk version: 0.8.2
2>  @0 < '/home/jallspaw/storage-consumption.xy'
15 points. No explicit std. dev. Set as sqrt(y)
3>  guess Quadratic
New function %_1 was created.
4>  fit
Initial values:  lambda=0.001  WSSR=464.564
#1:  WSSR=0.90162  lambda=0.0001  d(WSSR)=-463.663  (99.8059%)
#2:  WSSR=0.736787  lambda=1e-05  d(WSSR)=-0.164833  (18.2818%)
#3:  WSSR=0.736763  lambda=1e-06  d(WSSR)=-2.45151e-05  (0.00332729%)
#4:  WSSR=0.736763  lambda=1e-07  d(WSSR)=-3.84524e-11  (5.21909e-09%)
Fit converged.
Better fit found (WSSR = 0.736763, was 464.564, -99.8414%).
5> info formula in @0
# storage-consumption
14147.4+146.657*x+0.786854*x^2
6> quit

bye...
```

We now have our formula to fit the data:

$$0.786854x^2 + 146.657x + 14147.4$$

Note how the result looks almost exactly as Excel's for the same type of curve. Treating the values for x as days and those for y as our increasing disk space, we can plug in our 25-day forecast, which yields the same results as the Excel exercise. Table 4-2 lists the results generated by cfityk.

Table 4-2. *Same forecast as curve-fit by cfityk*

	Date	Disk available (GB)	$y = 0.786854x^2 + 146.657x + 14147.4$
33	08/27	20480.00	19843.97
34	08/28	20480.00	20043.34
35	08/29	20480.00	20244.29
36	08/30	20480.00	20446.81

	Date	Disk available (GB)	$y = 0.786854x^2 + 146.657x + 14147.4$
37	08/31	20480.00	20650.91
38	09/01	20480.00	20856.58
39	09/02	20480.00	21063.83

Being able to perform curve-fitting with a cfityk script makes it possible for you to carry out forecasting on a daily or weekly basis within a cron job, which can be an essential building block for a capacity planning dashboard.

Safety Factors

Web capacity planning can borrow a few useful strategies from the older and better-researched work of mechanical, manufacturing, and structural engineering. These disciplines also need to base design and management considerations around resources and immutable limits. The design and construction of buildings, bridges, and automobiles obviously requires some intimate knowledge of the strength and durability of materials, the loads each component is expected to bear, and what their ultimate failure points are. Does this sound familiar? It should, because capacity planning for web operations shares many of those same considerations and concepts.

Under load, materials such as steel and concrete undergo physical stresses. Some have elastic properties that allow them to recover under light amounts of load, but fail under higher strains. The same concerns exist in servers, networks, or storage. When their resources reach certain critical levels—100 percent CPU or disk usage, for example—they fail. To preempt this failure, engineers apply what is known as a *factor of safety* to their design. Defined briefly, a factor of safety indicates some margin of resource allocated beyond the theoretical capacity of that resource, to allow for uncertainty in the usage.

Whereas safety factors in the case of mechanical or structural engineering are usually part of the design phase, in web operations they should be considered as an amount of available resources that one leaves aside, with respect to the ceilings established for each class of resource. This will enable those resources to absorb some amount of unexpected increased usage. Resources by which you should calculate safety factors include all those discussed in Chapter 3: CPU, disk, memory, network bandwidth, even entire hosts (if your enterprise runs a very large site). For example, in Chapter 3 we stipulated 85 percent CPU usage as our upper limit for web servers in order to reserve "enough headroom to handle occasional spikes." In this case, we're allowing a 15 percent margin of "safety." When making forecasts, we need to take these safety factors into account and adjust the ceiling values appropriately.

Why a 15 percent margin? Why not 10 or 20 percent? One safety factor is going to be somewhat of a slippery number or educated guess. Some resources, such as caching systems, can also tolerate spikes better than others, so you might want to be less conservative with a margin of safety. You should base the safety margins on "spikes" of usage that you have seen in the past. See Figure 4-14.

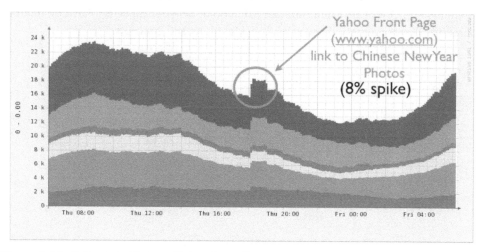

Figure 4-14. *Spike in traffic from Yahoo Front Page*

Figure 4-14 displays the effect of a typically sized traffic spike Flickr experiences on a regular basis. It's by no means the largest. Spikes such as this one almost always occur when the front page of yahoo.com posts a prominent link to a group, a photo, or a tag search page on Flickr. This particular spike was fleeting; it lasted only about two hours while the link was up. It caused an eight percent bump in traffic to Flickr's photo servers. Seeing a 5 to 15 percent increase in traffic like this is quite common, and confirms that our 15 percent margin of safety is adequate.

Procurement

As we've demonstrated, with our resource ceilings pinpointed, we can predict when we'll need more of a particular resource. When we complete the task of predicting when we'll need more, we can use that timeline to gauge when to trigger the procurement process.

The procurement pipeline is the process by which we obtain new capacity. It's usually the time it takes to justify, order, purchase, install, test, and deploy any new capacity. Figure 4-15 illustrates the procurement pipeline.

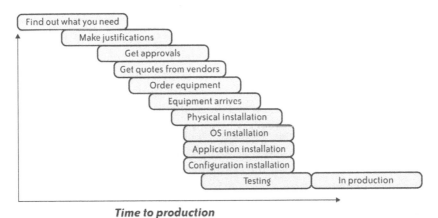

Time to production

Figure 4-15. *Typical procurement pipeline*

The tasks outlined in Figure 4-15 vary from one organization to another. In some large organizations, it can take a long time to gain approvals to buy hardware, but delivery can happen quickly. In a startup, approvals might come quickly, but the installation likely proceeds more slowly. Each situation will be different, but the challenge will remain the same: estimate how long the entire process will take, and add some amount of comfortable buffer to account for unforeseen problems. After you have an idea of what that buffer timeline is, you then can work backward to plan capacity.

Recall in our disk storage consumption example, we have current data on our disk consumption up to 8/15/05, and we estimate we'll run out of space on 8/30/05. Thus, there are exactly two weeks to justify, order, receive, install, and deploy new storage. If the timeline is not met, your storage capacity will run out and you will be forced to trim that consumption in some way. Ideally, this two-week deadline will be long enough to bring new capacity online.

Procurement Time: The Killer Metric

Obviously, the *when* of ordering equipment is just as important as the *what* and *how much*. Procurement timelines outlined earlier hint at how critical it is to keep an eye on how long it will take to get what is needed in production. Sometimes, external influences such as vendor delivery times and physical installation at the datacenter can ruin what started out to be a perfectly timed integration of new capacity.

Startups routinely order servers purely out of the fear that they'll be needed. Most newly launched companies have developers to work on the product and don't need to waste money on operations-focused engineers. The developers writing the code are most likely the same people setting up network switches, managing user accounts, installing software, and wearing whatever other hats are necessary to get their companies rolling. The last thing they want to worry about is running out of servers when they launch their new, awesome website. Ordering more servers as needed can be rightly justified in these cases because the hardware costs are more than offset by the costs of preparing a more streamlined and detailed capacity plan.

But as companies mature, optimizations begin to creep in. Code becomes more refined. The product becomes more defined. Marketing begins to realize who their users are. The same holds true for the capacity management process; it becomes more polished and accurate over time.

Just-in-Time Inventory

Toyota Motors developed the first implementations of a Just-in-Time (JIT) inventory practice. It knew there were large costs involved to organize, store, and track excess inventory of automobile parts, so it decided to reduce that "holding" inventory and determine exactly when it needed parts. Having inventory meant wasting money. Instead of maintaining a massive warehouse filled with the thousands of parts to make its cars, Toyota would order and stock only those parts as they were needed. This reduced costs tremendously and gave Toyota a competitive advantage in the 1950s. JIT inventory practice is now part of any modern manufacturing effort.

We can view the costs associated with having auto parts laying around in a warehouse as analogous to having servers installed before they are *really* needed. Rack space and power consumption in a datacenter cost money, as does the time spent installing and deploying code on the servers. More important, you risk suffering economically as a result of the aforementioned Moore's Law, which if the forecasts allow it, should motivate you to buy equipment later, rather than sooner.

As soon as you know when the current capacity will top out and how much capacity will be needed to get through to the next cycle of procurement, you should take a few lessons from the JIT inventory playbook, whose sole purpose it is to eliminate wastes of time and money in a given process.

Here are some of the steps in our typical procurement process that you should pay attention to and streamline:

1. Determine the needs

   By now, you should be able to assess how much load the current capacity can handle by following the advice given in Chapter 3 to find their ceilings, and you are measuring their usage constantly. Take these numbers to the curve-fitting table and begin making crystal ball predictions. This is fundamental to the capacity planning process.

2. Justify purchases

   Add some color and use attention-grabbing fonts on the graphs made in the previous step because these will be shown to the people who will approve the hardware purchases. Spend as much time as needed to ensure that the money-handling audience understands why the enterprise needs additional capacity, why it is needed now, and why more capacity will be needed going forward. Be very clear in the presentations about the downsides of insufficient capacity.

3. Solicit quotes from vendors

   Vendors want to sell servers and storage, and you want to buy servers and storage —all is balanced in the universe. On what basis should you choose vendor A over vendor B? Because vendor A might help alleviate some of the fear normally associated with ordering servers through such practices as quick turnarounds on quotes and replacements, discounts on servers ordered later, or discounts tied to delivery times.

4. Order equipment

   Can an order be tracked online? Is there a phone number (gasp!) for customer service who can tell you where the order is at all times? Does the datacenter know the machines are coming, and has the staff there factored that into their schedule?

5. Physical installation

How long will it take for the machines to make the journey from a loading dock into a rack and be cabled-up to a working switch? Does the datacenter staff need to get involved or are you racking servers yourself? Are there enough rack screws? Power drill batteries? Crossover cables? How long is this entire process going to take?

6. OS/application/configuration installation

In Chapter 5, we talk about deployment scenarios that involve automatic operating system OS installation, software deployment, and configuration management. However, just because it's automated doesn't mean it doesn't take time and that you shouldn't be aware of any problems that can arise.

7. Testing

Is there a QA team? Is there a QA environment? Testing an application means having some process by which you can functionally test all the bits to make sure everything is in its right place. Entire books are written on this topic; we would like to just remind you that it's a necessary step in the journey toward production life as a server.

8. Deploying new equipment

As the saying goes, it's not over until the fat server sings. Putting a machine into production should be straightforward. When doing so, you should use the same process to measure the capacity of the new servers as outlined in Chapter 3. Maybe you would want to ramp up the production traffic the machine receives by increasing its weight in the load-balanced pool. If this new capacity relieves a bottleneck, you would want to watch any effect that has on the traffic.

The Effects of Increasing Capacity

All of the segments within an infrastructure interact in various ways. Clients make requests to the web servers, which in turn make requests to databases, caching servers, storage, and all sorts of miscellaneous components. Layers of infrastructure work together to respond to users by providing web pages, pieces of web pages, or confirmations that they've performed some action, such as uploading a photo.

When one or more of those layers encounters a bottleneck, you need to determine how much more capacity is needed and then deploy it. Depending on how bottlenecked that layer or cluster is, you might observe second-order effects of that new deployment and end up simply moving the traffic jam to yet another part of the architecture. For example, let's assume that a website involves a web server and a database. One of the ways organizations can help scale their applications is to cache computationally expensive database results. Deploying something like *memcached* can facilitate this. In a nutshell, it means for certain database queries, you can consult an in-memory cache before accessing the database. This is done primarily for the dual purpose of speeding up the query and reducing load on the database server for results that are frequently returned.

The most noticeable benefit is that the queries that used to take seconds to process might take as little as a few milliseconds, which means a web server will be able to send the response to the client more quickly. Ironically, there's a side effect to this; when users are not waiting for pages as long, they have a tendency to click links faster, causing more load on the web servers. It's not uncommon to see memcached deployments turn into web server capacity issues rather quickly.

Long-Term Trends

By now, you should know how to apply the statistics collected in Chapter 3 to immediate needs. But you also might want to view a site from a more global perspective—both in the literal sense (as a site becomes popular internationally), and in a figurative sense, as you look at the issues surrounding the product and the site's strategy.

Traffic Pattern Changes

As mentioned earlier, getting to know the peaks and valleys of the various resources and application usage is paramount to predicting the future. As you gain more and more history with the metrics, you might be able to perceive more subtle trends that will inform the long-term decisions. For example, let's take a look at Figure 4-16, which illustrates a typical traffic pattern for a web server.

Figure 4-16 shows a pretty typical daily traffic pattern in the United States. The load rises slowly in the morning, East Coast time, as users begin browsing. These users go to lunch as West Coast users come online, keeping up the load, which finally drops off as people leave work. At this point, the load drops to only those users browsing overnight.

As usage grows, you can expect this graph to grow vertically as more users visit the site during the same peaks and valleys. But if the audience grows more internationally, the bump you would see every day will widen as the number of active user time zones increases. As illustrated in Figure 4-17, you even might see distinct bumps after the US drop-off if the site's popularity grows in a region further away than Europe.

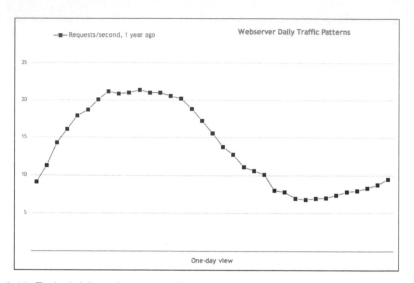

Figure 4-16. *Typical daily web server traffic pattern*

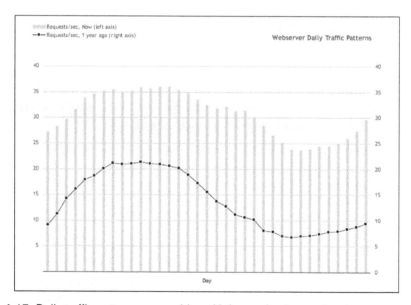

Figure 4-17. *Daily traffic patterns grow wider with increasing international usage*

Figure 4-17 displays two daily traffic patterns, taken one year apart, and superimposed one atop the other. What once was a smooth bump and decline has become a two-peak bump, due to the global effect of popularity.

Of course, the product and marketing people are probably very aware of the demographics and geographic distribution of the audience, but tying this data to a system's resources can help you to predict the capacity needs.

Forecasting Considerations for Multiple Datacenters

When a site's growth dictates serving content out of multiple datacenters, you might notice certain geographic traffic patterns can emerge that might not be seen with a single datacenter. When we were at Flickr, the datacenters in the United States were split between the east and west coasts, and content was served to the users from the geographically closest datacenter. Photos were distributed into what were referred to as *photo farms*. A farm was made up of a mirrored pair of datacenters, one on each coast, and each farm contained a unique set of photos. Photos were stored in the two locations for redundancy, in the event of emergency, or if one of a farm's datacenters needed to be taken offline for maintenance.

At the launch of the second location, it was observed that the east coast datacenter received as much as 65 to 70 percent more traffic at peak than its west coast counterpart. This was easily explained: at the time the European users were a much more engaged audience than the Asian users, and because the US east coast is closer to Europe, the usage was commensurately higher. In addition, it was noticed that the west coast datacenters received considerably more requests for the larger, original sizes of photos than the east coast. This, in part, was attributed to home broadband connections in Asia having higher bandwidth limits, so the users in Asia were accustomed to downloading larger amounts of data.

What this meant was that the peaks and valleys differed for each side of each farm, and therefore the forecasts needed to be adjusted during capacity planning. As just mentioned, the architecture for each datacenter in a farm dictated that it must be able to handle 100 percent of the traffic for entire farm in the event its partner datacenter falls out of operation. Therefore, capacity forecasts need to be based on the cumulative peaks of both datacenters in a farm.

As we alluded to in Chapter 3, when you deploy capacity to multiple datacenters, usage patterns can become more complex. You would need to take that into consideration when forecasting capacity.

Figure 4-17 also shows that the web servers must sustain their peak traffic for longer periods of time. This will indicate when any maintenance windows should be scheduled to minimize the effect of downtime or degraded service to the users. Notice the ratio between the peak and low period has changed, as well. This will affect how many servers you can tolerate losing to failure during those periods, which is effectively the ceiling of a cluster.

It's important to watch the change in an application's traffic pattern, not only for operational issues, but to drive capacity decisions, such as whether to deploy any capacity to international datacenters.

Application Usage Changes and Product Planning

A good capacity plan relies not only on system statistics such as peaks and valleys, but user behavior, as well. How users interact with the site is yet another valuable vein of data that you should mine for information to help keep the crystal ball as clear as possible.

If you run an online community, you might have discussion boards in which users create new topics, make comments, and upload media such as video and photos. In addition to the previously discussed system-related metrics such as storage consumption, video- and photo-processing CPU usage, and processing time, here are some other metrics you might want to track:

- Discussion posts per minute
- Posts per day, per user
- Video uploads per day, per user
- Photo uploads per day, per user

Application usage is just another way of saying *user engagement*, to borrow a term from the product and marketing folks.

Recall back to our database-planning example. In that example, we found our database ceiling by measuring our hardware's resources (CPU, disk I/O, memory, etc.), relating them to the database's resources (queries per second, replication lag), and tying those ceilings to something we can measure from the user interaction perspective (how many photos per user are on each database).

This is where capacity planning and product management tie together. Using system and application statistics histories, we can now predict with some (hopefully increasing) degree of accuracy what we would need to meet future demand. But, again, history is only part of the picture. If the product team is planning new features, you can bet that they'll affect the capacity plan in some way.

Historically, corporate culture has isolated product development from engineering. Product people develop ideas and plans for the product, whereas engineering develops and maintains the product after it's on the market. Both groups make forecasts for different ends, but the data used in those forecasts should tie together.

One of the best practices for a capacity planner is to develop an ongoing conversation with product management. Understanding the timeline for new features is critical to guaranteeing capacity needs don't interfere with product improvements. Having enough capacity is an engineering requirement, in the same way development time and resources are.

Iteration and Calibration

Producing forecasts by curve-fitting the system and application data isn't the end of capacity planning. To make it accurate, you need to revisit the plan, refit the data, and adjust accordingly.

Ideally, you should have periodic reviews of the forecasts. You should check how the capacity is doing against the predictions on a weekly, or even daily, basis. If you are nearing capacity on one or more resources and are awaiting delivery of new hardware, you might keep a much closer eye on it. The important thing to remember is that the plan will be accurate only if you consistently reexamine the trends and question the past predictions.

As an example, we can revisit our simple storage consumption data. We made a forecast based on data we gleaned for a 15-day period, from 7/26/05 to 8/09/05. We also discovered that on 8/30/05 (roughly two weeks later), we expected to run out of space if we didn't deploy more storage. More accurately, we were slated to reach 20,446.81 GB of space, which would have exceeded our total available space, which is 20,480 GB. How accurate was that prediction? Figure 4-18 shows what actually happened.

As it turned out, we had a little more time than we thought—about four days more. We made a guess based on the trend at the time, which ended up being inaccurate but at least in favor of allowing more time to integrate new capacity. Sometimes, forecasts can either widen the window of time (as in this case) or narrow it. This is why the process of revisiting the forecasts is critical; it's the only way to adjust the capacity plan over time. Every time you update the capacity plan, you should go back and evaluate how the previous forecasts fared.

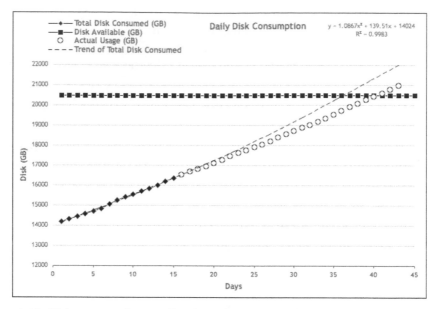

Figure 4-18. *Disk consumption: predicted trend versus actual*

Given that curve-fitting and trending results tend to improve as you add more data points, you should have a moving window to make forecasts. The width of that forecasting window will vary depending on how long the procurement process takes. For example, if you know that it's going to take three months on average to order, install, and deploy capacity, you would want the forecast goal to be three months out, each time. As the months pass, you would want to add the influence of most recent events to the past data and to recompute the predictions, as is illustrated in Figure 4-19.

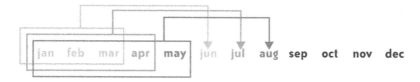

Figure 4-19. *A moving window of forecasts*

Best Guesses

This process of plotting, prediction, and iteration can provide a lot of confidence in how to manage the capacity. You would have accumulated a lot of data about how the current infrastructure is performing and how close each piece is to their respective ceilings, taking into account comfortable margins of safety. This confidence is important because the capacity planning process (as we've seen) is just as much about educated guessing and luck as it is about hard science and math. Hopefully, the iterations in the planning process will point out any flawed assumptions in the working data, but it should also be said that the ceilings you are using could become flawed or obsolete over time, as well.

Just as the ceilings can change depending on the hardware specifications of a server, so too can the actual metric that you are assuming as the ceiling. For example, the defining metric of a database might be disk I/O, but after upgrading to a newer and faster disk subsystem, you might find the limiting factor isn't disk I/O anymore, but the single gigabit network card you're using. It bears mentioning that picking the right metric to follow can be difficult because not all bottlenecks are obvious, and the metric you choose can change as the architecture and hardware limitations change.

During this process, you might notice seasonal variations. College starts in the fall, so there might be increased usage as students browse the site for materials related to their studies (or just to avoid going to class). As another example, the holiday season in November and December almost always witnesses a bump in traffic, especially for sites involving retail sales. At Flickr, we saw both of those seasonal effects.

Taking into account these seasonal or holiday variations should be yet another influence on how wide or narrow the forecasting window might be. Obviously, the more often you recalculate a forecast, the better prepared you would be, and the sooner you would notice unexpected variations.

Diagonal Scaling Opportunities

As we pointed out near the beginning of the chapter, predicting capacity requires two essential bits of information: the ceilings and the historical data. The historical data is etched in stone. The ceilings are not, because each ceiling is indicative of a particular hardware configuration. Performance tuning can hopefully change those ceilings for the better, but upgrading the hardware to newer and better technology is also an option.

As we mentioned at the beginning of the book, new technology can dramatically change how much horsepower you can squeeze from a single server. The forecasting process shown in this chapter allows you to not only track where you're headed on a per-node basis, but also to think about which segments of the architecture you might possibly move to new hardware options.

Summary

Predicting capacity is an ongoing process that requires as much intuition as it does math to help one make accurate forecasts. Even simple web applications need to be attended, and some of this crystal-ball work can be tedious. Automating as much of the process as you can will help you to stay ahead of the procurement process. Taking the time to connect the metric collection systems to trending software, such as cfityk, will prove to be invaluable as you develop a capacity plan that is easily adaptable. Ideally, you would want some sort of a capacity dashboard that can be referred to at any point in time to inform purchasing, development, and operational decisions.

The overall process in making capacity forecasts is pretty simple:

1. Determine, measure, and graph the defining metric for each resource.

   Example: disk consumption

2. Apply the constraints to each resource.

   Example: total available disk space

3. Use trending analysis (curve-fitting) to illustrate when the usage will exceed the constraint.

   Example: find the day when you will run out of disk space

Readings

1. G. E. Moore. (1965). *Cramming More Components onto Integrated Circuits*.
2. M. A. Cusumano and D. B. Yoffie. (2016). *Extrapolating from Moore's Law*.
3. P. E. Denning and T. G. Lewis. (2017). *Exponential Laws of Computing Growth*.

Buy or Lease

1. R. F. Vancil. (1961). *Lease or Borrow: New Method of Analysis*.

2. K. D. Ripley. (1962). *Leasing: a means of financing that business should not overlook*.

3. R. W. Johnson. (1972). *Analysis of the Lease-or-Buy Decision*.

4. W. L. Sartoris and R. S. Paul. (1973). *Lease Evaluation: Another Capital Budgeting Decision*.

5. G. B. Harwood and R. H. Hermanson. (1976). *Lease-or-Buy Decisions*.

6. A. Sykes. (1976). *The Lease-Buy Decision - A Survey of Current Practice in 202 Companies*.

7. Jack E. Gaumnitz and Allen Ford. (1978). *The Lease or Sell Decision*.

8. A. C. C. Herst. (1984). *Lease or Purchase: Theory and Practice*.

9. B. H. Nunnally, J. R. and D. A. Plath. (1989). *Leasing Versus Borrowing: Evaluating Alternative Forms of Consumer Credit*.

10. F. J. Fabozzi. (2008). *Lease versus Borrow-to-Buy Analysis*.

11. E. Walker. (2009). *The Real Cost of a CPU Hour*.

12. E. Walker et al. (2010). *To Lease or Not to Lease from Storage Clouds*.

Time–Series Forecasting

1. G. E. P. Box, et al. (2015). *Time–Series Analysis: Forecasting and Control* (5th ed.).

2. P. J. Brockwell and R. A. Davis. (2002). *Introduction to Time Series and Forecasting* (2nd ed.).

Curve Fitting

1. G. Wabba. (1990). *Spline Models for Observational Data*.

2. S. Arlinghaus. (1994). *Practical Handbook of Curve Fitting*.

3. G. D. Garson. (2012). *Curve Fitting and Non-linear Regression*.

Measurement

1. Y. Zhang, et al. (2016). *Treadmill: Attributing the Source of Tail Latency through Precise Load Testing and Statistical Inference*.

Resources

1. "Moore's Law Is Dead. Now What?" (2016) *http://bit.ly/moores-law-dead*.

2. L. Muehlhauser. (2014). *Exponential and non-exponential trends in information technology* (*https://intelligence.org/2014/05/12/exponential-and-non-exponential/*).

## CHAPTER FIVE

Deployment

After you have an idea of how much capacity is needed for future growth and have purchased the hardware, you need to deploy it into production. In the case of a cloud setup, this entails configuring autoscaling (this is discussed in depth in Chapter 6). conversely, for a datacenter (which can be a managed service, as well), this also entails physically installing the hardware.

Historically, deployment has been viewed as a headache. Installing the operating system and application software, ensuring that all of the right settings are in place, and loading a website's data—all of these tedious steps must be done to integrate the new instances in the cloud, or new hardware that's fresh out of the crate in a datacenter. Fortunately, the pain of repeating these steps over and over has inspired an entire category of software: automated installation and configuration tools such as Vagrant, Chef, Puppet, Pallet, Ansible, and CFEngine.[1] This new category of tools is commonly talked about under the umbrella of *infrastructure as code*, or *programmable infrastructure*.

---

1 A part of this chapter was written by John's former colleague at Flickr, Kevin Murphy.

In essence, infrastructure as code refers to writing code (which you can do using a high-level language or any descriptive language) to manage configurations and automate provisioning of infrastructure in addition to deployments. It differs from *infrastructure automation*, which just involves replicating steps multiple times and reproducing them on several servers.

Automated Deployment Philosophies

Although various automatic installation and configuration tools differ in their implementation and execution, most of them share the same design philosophy. Just as with monitoring and metric-collection tools, many of these concepts and designs originated in the high-performance computing (HPC) field. Because HPC and web operations have similarities in their infrastructure, the web operations community has adopted many of these tools and approaches. In this section, we briefly outline the key goals and what each entails.

Goal 1: Minimize Time to Provision New Capacity

When you are trying to determine when your capacity is going to run out, you must factor into the calculations the time needed to acquire, install, and provision new hardware. If the capacity will be exhausted in six weeks, and it takes three weeks to add new hardware, you have only three weeks of breathing room. Automated deployment and configuration minimizes the time spent on the phase of the process over which you have the most control—integrating machines onto the network and beginning operations. A key aspect to this end is to have a homogeneous hardware (see the sidebar for further discussion).

Goal 2: All Changes Happen in One Place

When you're making changes to hosts, it's preferable to have a central location from which to push changes appropriate to the servers that you are affecting. Having a central location provides a "control tower" from which to manage all aspects of the infrastructure. Unlike server architectures, in which distributed resources help with horizontal scaling, centralized configuration and management environments yield several advantages:

- You can employ version control for all configurations: operating system (OS), application, or otherwise. You can use Git, Perforce, RCS, CVS, Subversion, and so on to track the "who, what, when, and why" of each change to the infrastructure.

- Replication and backup of installation and configuration files is easier to manage.

- An aggregated configuration and management logging system is an ideal troubleshooting resource.

- This centralized management environment makes an ideal place to keep hardware inventory, particularly if you want to have different configuration settings for different hardware.

This is not to suggest that your configuration, installation, monitoring, and management setup should be kept on a single server. Each of these deployment components demands specific resources. Growth over time would simply overwhelm a single machine, rendering it a potential single point of failure. Separate these components from the rest of the infrastructure. Monitoring and metric collection can reside on one server; configuration management and log aggregation on another. Figure 5-1 presents an example of a typical installation, configuration, and management architecture.

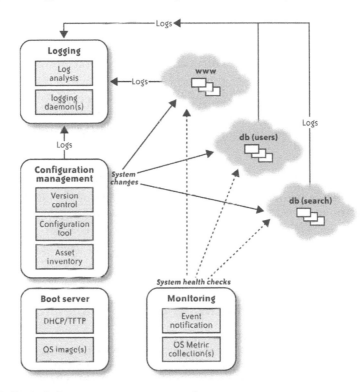

Figure 5-1. *Typical cluster management scenario*

Goal 3: Never Log in to an Individual Server (for Management)

Restrict logging in to an individual server to troubleshooting or forensic work only. All configuration or management should be done from the centralized management servers. This keeps the production changes in an auditable and controlled environment.

Goal 4: Have New Servers Start Working Automatically

This is the holy grail of all deployment systems. You should be able to order hardware, add it to the inventory-management system, turn it on, have it automatically install all required software and register itself with the monitoring systems, and then get down to work, all without administrator intervention.

Goal 5: Maintain Consistency for Easier Troubleshooting

Coordination of troubleshooting efforts during outages or emergencies is critical. Configuration management tools effectively enable that coordination. Consistent OS and software configuration across a cluster of identically deployed servers eliminates configuration inconsistencies as a source of problems. Troubleshooting in large production environments is difficult enough without needing to isolate configuration discrepancies between a handful of servers. Further, having disparate software configurations across nodes in a given cluster can potentially hinder performance optimization. For instance, having different versions of the gcc compiler can limit application of certain compiler optimizations as a result of certain optimizations not being supported in older versions. In a similar version, having different versions of the Java Development Kit (JDK) might limit the application of certain Just-in-Time (JIT) optimizations by the Java HotSpot compiler.

When tracking down a bug, the ability to quickly view all of the changes that occurred between the last known good state and the present (bad) state can be invaluable. When more than one person is working on an issue, a centralized and consistent overview of all of the changes is crucial. With version control, changes are immediately apparent and tasks aren't repeated. Nor are they assumed to have been completed or otherwise mixed up with other tasks.

Homogenize Hardware to Halt Headaches

In addition to making software configurations consistent between servers that perform the same role, it's valuable to have consistency at the hardware level, as well. Back at Flickr, we had two basic server types: a multiple-disk machine for I/O-intensive tasks, and a single-disk machine for CPU-intensive jobs (for which most of the working set fits in memory). Limiting the number of hardware types has a number of advantages:

- It reduces variability between machines, which simplifies troubleshooting.

- In the case of a datacenter, it minimizes the number of different spare parts your organization needs to keep on hand and facilitates cannibalizing dead machines for parts.

- It simplifies automated deployment and configuration because you don't need to create numerous special-case configurations for different hardware.

"Today's theme is 'Getting Beyond Group Think'."

Virtualized infrastructures can take this a step further. You can buy racks of identical servers and allocate memory, CPU, and high performance remote storage to virtual machines (VMs) based on application need.

Having said all of this, to boost performance, increasingly graphics processing units (GPUs) are being used for a variety of tasks. Consequently, popular public cloud vendors offer GPU-based instance types such as P2 and G2 instance types on Amazon Web Services (AWS). Amazon EC2 Elastic GPUs make it possible for you to easily attach low-cost graphics acceleration to current generation EC2 instances. With Elastic GPUs, you can choose the GPU resources that are sized for the workload at hand, so one can accelerate the graphics performance of your applications. Use of Elastic GPUs can be beneficial if you need a small amount of GPU for graphics acceleration or have applications that could benefit from some GPU but also require high amounts of compute, memory, or storage.

In a similar manner, with Deep Learning gaining traction, instance types with field-programmable gate arrays (FPGAs) are being supported. This is exemplified by the Amazon EC2 F1 instance type. In May 2016, Google announced that it uses a custom application-specific integrated circuit (ASIC) called Tensor Processing Unit (TPU)—tailored for TensorFlow—in its datacenters, and has found TPUs to deliver an order of magnitude better-optimized performance per watt for machine learning.

As new application domains arise, it's quite likely that the hardware, be it cloud or on-premises, would organically become more and more heterogeneous. This calls for constant innovation on the infrastructure-as-code front.

Automated Installation Tools

Before you can begin to even think about configuration management, you need to get the servers to a state in which they can be configured. You want a system that can automatically (and repetitively) install the OS of choice. Many such systems have been developed over the years, all employing similar techniques.

There are two basic approaches to the task of imaging new machines. Most OS vendors offer a package-based installer option, which performs the normal installation process in a noninteractive fashion. It provides the installer with a configuration file that specifies the packages to be installed. Examples include Solaris Jumpstart, Red Hat Kickstart, and Debian FAI.

Many third-party products take a *disk-image approach*. A *gold client* image is prepared on one machine and replicated byte-for-byte onto newly imaged hosts. Often, a single image is used for every server in the infrastructure, with hosts differing only in the services that are configured and running. SystemImager is a product that uses this approach.

Each method—package-based versus image-based—has its own advantages. Package-based systems provide accountability; every file installed is guaranteed to belong to a package, and package management tools make it easy to quickly see what's installed. You can achieve the same result with disk-image systems by installing only packaged files. The temptation to muck about with the gold client filesystem directly can lead to confusion down the road. On the other hand, image-based systems tend to be faster to install. The installer merely has to create a filesystem and dump the image onto it, rather than download many packages, calculate dependencies, and install them one by one. Some products such as SystemImager even support parallel installs to multiple clients by streaming the disk images via multicast or BitTorrent.

On AWS, an Amazon Machine Image (AMI) is specified to launch one or more instances. An AMI includes the following:

- A template for the root volume for the instance (for example, an OS, an application server, and applications)
- Launch permissions that control which AWS accounts can use the AMI to launch instances
- A block device mapping that specifies the volumes to attach to the instance when it's launched

You can copy an AMI to the same region or to different regions. After launching an instance from an AMI, you can deregister the AMI. In fact, there is a marketplace for AMI where users can buy, share, and sell AMIs. An AMI is categorized as either backed by Amazon Elastic Block Store (EBS) or backed by instance store. The former means that the root device for an instance launched from the AMI is an Amazon EBS volume created from an Amazon EBS snapshot. The latter means that the root device for an instance launched from the AMI is an instance store volume created from a template stored in Amazon S3 (for references to details about AMIs, go to "Resources" on page 154). Figure 5-2 illustrates the life cycle of an AMI.

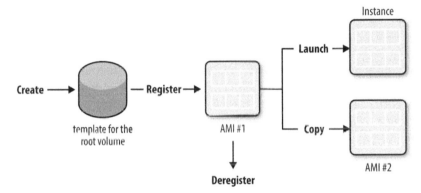

Figure 5-2. *Life cycle of an AMI*

At Netflix, to minimize the application startup latency, AMIs were designed to be discrete and complete, as demonstrated in Figure 5-3. First, using a standard Linux distribution such as Ubuntu or CentOS, a foundation AMI was created. An empty EBS volume was mounted, a filesystem was then created, a minimal OS was installed, a snapshot of the AMI was taken, and then, finally, the AMI was registered based on the snapshot.

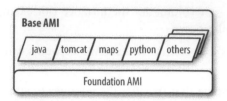

Figure 5-3. *An example Base AMI*

The base AMI then was constructed by mounting an EBS volume created from the foundation AMI snapshot. Next it was customized with a meta package (RPM or DEB) that, through dependencies, pulled in other packages that comprised the Netflix base AMI. This volume was dismounted, snapshotted, and then registered as a candidate base AMI, which made it available for building application AMIs. In March 2013, Netflix announced the tool called *Aminator* to create custom machine images on AWS.

NOTE

For a reference to details about *Aminator*, go to "Resources" on page 154.

Linux AMIs use one of two types of virtualization: paravirtual (PV) or hardware VM (HVM). The two main differences between PV and HVM AMIs are the way in which they boot and whether they can take advantage of special hardware extensions (CPU, network, and storage) for better performance. PV AMIs boot with a special boot loader called PV-GRUB, which starts the boot cycle and then chain-loads the kernel specified in the *menu.lst* file on the image. Paravirtual guests can run on host hardware that does not have explicit support for virtualization, but they cannot take advantage of special hardware extensions such as enhanced networking or GPU processing. Historically, PV guests had better performance than HVM guests in many cases, but because of enhancements in HVM virtualization and the availability of PV drivers for HVM AMIs, this is no longer true. On the other hand, HVM AMIs exploit a fully virtualized set of hardware and boot by executing the master boot record of the root block device of the image. This virtualization type provides the ability to run an operating system directly on top of a VM without any modification, as if it were run on the bare-metal hardware. The Amazon EC2 host system emulates some or all of the underlying hardware that is presented to the guest. Unlike PV guests, HVM guests can take advantage of hardware extensions that provide fast access to the underlying hardware on the host system.

Figure 5-4 depicts the life cyle of an instance on AWS (note that the life cycle is similar on other public clouds).

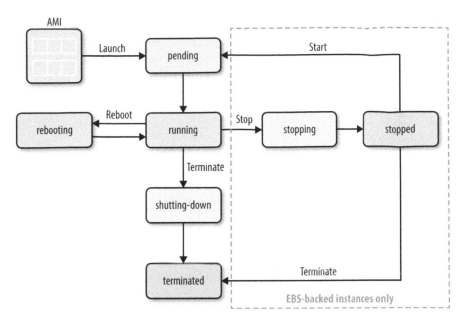

Figure 5-4. *Life cycle of an instance on AWS*

Preparing the OS Image

In a cloud context, a rich set of tools are provided by the cloud vendor to install a basic version of the OS of choice and then install the required packages. However, in the on-premises context, most organizations aren't happy with the OS their vendor installs. Default OS installations are notoriously inappropriate for production environments because they are designed to run on as many different hardware platforms as possible. They usually contain packages that you don't need and typically are missing those that you do. As a result, most companies create custom OS images suitable for their specific needs.

For a package-based system, the OS image is specified by preparing a configuration file that lists the set of packages to be installed. You can simply dump the package list from an existing server and tweak it as desired. Then, you put the configuration file in the appropriate place on the boot server, and it's all set. On the other hand, for an image-based system, it's slightly more involved. Normally, a server is set aside to be the gold client that provides the template for the deployed image. This can be a physical server set aside for the purpose, or even a VM. You perform a normal OS installation and install all the software required in the infrastructure. The client image then is copied to the deployed server.

The Installation Process

If you are installing more than a handful of machines, installations with physical boot media such as CD-ROMs quickly become tedious and require someone to be physically present at the datacenter. You are going to want to set up a network boot server, which in the case of PC hardware usually means a Pre-Boot Execution Environment (PXE), as shown in Figure 5-5.

Figure 5-5. *Basic steps of the PXE booting process*

PXE-based installations are performed by a number of services working together. PXE firmware on the client requests its environment via Dynamic Host Configuration Protocol (DHCP). A DHCP server provides the information required to fetch the boot image (IP address, boot server, and image name). Finally, the client fetches the boot image from the boot server via TFTP.

For automated installation systems, the boot image consists of a kernel, plus a ramdisk containing the installer program. (This differs from diskless client setups, for which the boot image contains the production kernel the client uses to mount a network volume as its root filesystem.) The installer then determines what type of host is being installed and formats the local filesystems appropriately. There are several methods for mapping hardware profiles to hosts; typically they involve assigning configurations based on a hostname or a MAC address. For example, Kickstart passes the configuration filename as part of the DHCP options and fetches it from the Trivial File Transfer Protocol (TFTP) server, whereas SystemImager has a configuration file stored on the image server that maps image types to hostnames. The installer then installs the OS from the network onto the newly formatted volumes. As it pertains to a package-based installer, this means copying package files from a network repository (for example, apt or yum). For image-based systems, the OS image is dumped directly onto the local volumes, usually via rsync or a similar program.

After the OS image is installed, the PXE server marks the host as installed. Typically, this is done by replacing the host's bootfile with a stub that instructs the host to boot from the local disk. The machine is restarted and boots normally. As shipped, most automated deployment systems require some manual configuration. You need to create DHCP server configurations and map hostnames to roles. However, inventory management systems should have all the information about a machine required to boot it: MAC address, role, IP address, and hostname. With a bit of clever scripting, you can generate the required configuration automatically from the asset database.

After this is set up, provisioning new servers is as simple as entering their details into inventory management, racking them, and powering them up. Reformatting a machine is as simple as assigning it a new role in the database and rebooting it. (Normally, a reinstallation is required only if the disk layout changes. Otherwise, you simply can reconfigure the server.)

The deployment beast has been tamed!

Automated Configuration

Now that the machines are up on the network, it's time to configure them to do their jobs. Configuration management systems help with this task in the following ways:

- They let you organize the configuration files into useful subsystems, which you can combine in various ways to build production systems.
- They put all the information about the running systems in one place, from which it easily can be backed-up or replicated to another site or property of the same site.
- They extract institutional knowledge out of an administrator's head and place it into a form that can be documented and reused.

A typical configuration management system consists of a server in which configurations are stored, and a client process, which runs on each host and requests a configuration from the server. In an infrastructure with automated deployment, the client is run as part of the initial installation or immediately after the initial boot into the new OS. After the initial configuration, a scheduled task on the client host periodically polls the server to see if any new configuration is available. Automating these checks ensures that every machine in an infrastructure is always running the latest configuration.

As mentioned earlier, several configuration tools have been developed over the years. Examples include Chef, Puppet, Ansible, CFEngine, SaltStack.

NOTE ————————————————————————————————
For references to books on the subject, go to "Readings" on page 153.

Defining Roles and Services

You have a shiny new configuration management system installed. Now, how do you actually use it? The best way to attack the problem is to divide and conquer. *Services* (collections of related software and configurations) are the atoms, and *roles* (the types of machines in an infrastructure) are the molecules. Examples of a service and a role are discussed later in this section. After a robust set of services is defined, it is straightforward to shuffle existing services into alternative combinations to serve new roles or to split an existing role into more specialized configurations.

First, go through all of the machines in the infrastructure (or planned infrastructure) and identify the present roles. A role is a particular type of machine that performs a particular task. For a website, a list might include roles such as a "web server" and a "database." Next, go through each role and determine which services need to be present on each instance of the role for the instance to be able to do its job. A service in this sense is not just an OS-level program like httpd. For example, the HTTP server service would include not only the httpd package and its configuration, but also settings for any metrics, health checks, or associated software that runs on a machine serving web pages.

As you go through the various roles, try to identify services that might be common to multiple roles. For example, every server is likely to require a remote login service such as sshd. By identifying these common services, you can create a single set of configuration routines that you can use over and over for deploying current as well as new roles that might emerge as the site grows.

An Example: Splitting Off Static Web Content

Suppose that you have a cluster of four web servers. Each machine serves a combination of static content and dynamic pages generated by PHP. Apache's MaxClients setting is tuned down to 80 simultaneous connections to ensure that the machines don't overrun available memory and initiate swapping. The web server role might look similar to Figure 5-6.

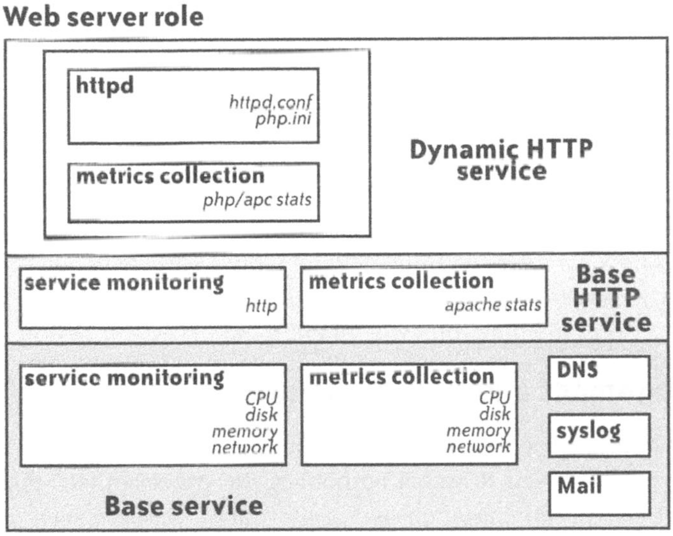

Web server role

Figure 5-6. *The web server role and associated services*

You might realize in a flash of insight that more simultaneous clients can be served by splitting the cluster into two roles: one with the current configuration for dynamic content, and one with a stripped-down Apache with a larger MaxClients to serve only static content. To this end, first, you would split out services common to both roles into a separate service called base_http. This service includes settings that any web server should have, such as an HTTP health check and metrics pulled from Apache's status module. Next, you would create two new services. The dynamic HTTP service contains the original Apache and PHP configurations. The static HTTP service is configured with a simplified *httpd.conf* with a larger client cap and no PHP module. Then, roles are defined for each server type by combining these services. Figure 5-7 depicts the new roles.

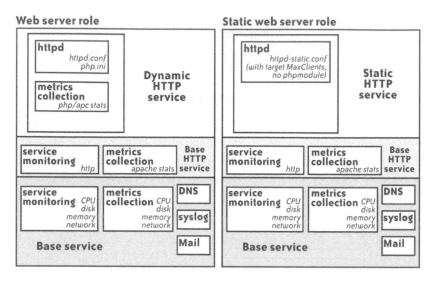

Figure 5-7. *Static web server role and associated services*

Now that the new role is defined, you can either go into the inventory management system and assign one or more existing web server machines to the static_webserver role, or deploy new hardware with the new role. If you decide to add more metrics or health checks, which are applicable to both roles in the future, you can put them in the base_http service, and both roles will inherit them.

User Management and Access Control

User management and access control require special consideration. How do you control which users have access to which portions of the system In fact, there are several ways. Network-based authentication and authorization services such as Lightweight Directory Access Protocol (LDAP) are popular. Users and groups can be granted access to individual machines or host groups in one place. Permission and password changes are propagated automatically. On the downside, these systems represent yet another service that needs to be provisioned, monitored, and scaled as the infrastructure grows.

Alternatively, it's possible to use a configuration management system to install user accounts on a host or role basis by defining services that make the appropriate changes to the system authentication databases. This is straightforward if you already have configuration management in place. However, with such a system, password changes and access additions and revocations cannot be applied to all servers simultaneously. Additionally, if automated configuration updates are broken on a host, that host might not receive the latest access configuration at all, which is an obvious security concern.

Both of these setups can be made to work. Which one is most appropriate for the infrastructure depends on the existing authentication systems, the number of users involved, and the frequency with which changes are made. If you are already using LDAP elsewhere in the organization, that might be the natural choice. If you have a small number of users and changes are infrequent, a package-based system might be appropriate.

Ad Hockery

By now, you should have a good grasp about configuration management—an infrastructure full of properly configured servers that you would never need to log in to in order to manage it. But what if you want to? There are times when you might like to log into all of the members of a particular role and run a command. Fortunately, there are tools to make this task easier. These tools run the gamut from simple "run ssh in a for loop" scripts, to sophisticated remote scripting systems, like `Capistrano`.

Ideally, such a tool should integrate with the configuration management system. Still, you might want to be able to log in to groups of servers by role, or even by service. This might require some scripting to convert the role and service definitions into a format the tool understands. Alternatively, the tool might be provided as a component of the configuration management or monitoring system (such as the `gexec` utility provided with Ganglia).

You can run commands on multiple servers. But should you? In general, a good use for these utilities is to gather ad hoc data about the systems—perhaps information you're not measuring with the trending tools. They're also useful for debugging and forensics. The rule of thumb should be: If it's not something that you should be collecting as a metric, and it won't affect server state, it's OK.

When is it a bad idea? You should hesitate any time it would be more appropriate to use configuration management. There's always the possibility of forgetting ad hoc changes. You will regret forgetting.

Example 2: Multiple Datacenters

Eventually, you would want to attack the greatest single point of failure of them all—the cloud or the on-premises datacenter. You would want to be able to continue to serve traffic even if the cloud or the datacenter experiences a catastrophic power failure or other calamity. When you expand the infrastructure into multiple physical sites, you begin to realize the gains of automation on an even larger scale. Besides disaster recovery, geographically distributed cloud sites or on-premises datacenters are used to augment the end-user experience by minimizing the "wire time." Big companies such as Amazon, Google, Facebook, Twitter, and Microsoft have multiple datacenters around the globe. In a similar vein, Netflix has its service set up across different AWS regions around the world.

Bringing up another datacenter can look like a logistical nightmare on paper. It took months or years to get the current systems in place. How would you be able to rebuild them in another location quickly? Automated deployment can make the prospect of bringing up an entire facility from bare metal much less daunting.

Rather than replicate each system in the original site on a host-by-host basis, the process unfolds as such:

- Set up management hosts in the new datacenter. The base installs might be manual, but the configuration is not—the management host configurations should be in configuration management, as well!

- Tweak the base configurations to suit the new environment. For example, DNS configuration and routing information will differ.

- Allocate roles to the new machines on the boot server (or in inventory management).

- Boot the hosts and allow them to install and configure themselves.

To simplify synchronization of settings between datacenters, it's best to keep all datacenter-specific configurations in a separate service or set of services. This makes it possible for you to attain maximum reuse out of the service definitions.

Summary

Knowing how much hardware you need does little good if you can't get that hardware into service quickly. Automating the infrastructure with tools like configuration management and automated installation ensures that the deployment processes are efficient and repeatable. Automation converts system administration tasks from one-off efforts into reusable building blocks.

Readings

1. K. Morris. *Infrastructure as Code*.

2. M. Taylor and S. Vargo. (2014). *Learning Chef: A Guide to Configuration Management and Automation*.

3. M. Marschall. (2015). *Chef Infrastructure Automation Cookbook*.

4. L. Hochstein. (2014). *Ansible: Up and Running, Automating Configuration Management and Deployment the Easy Way*.

5. P. Duvall et al. *Continuous Integration: Improving Software Quality and Reducing Risk*.

6. J. Humble and D. Farley. *Continuous Delivery: Reliable Software Releases through Build, Test, and Deployment Automation*.

7. N. Ford. *Engineering Practices for Continuous Delivery: From Metrics and Deployment Pipelines to Integration and Microservices*.

Resources

1. "Infrastructure as Code: A Reason to Smile." (2016) *https://www.thoughtworks.com/insights/blog/infrastructure-code-reason-smile*.

2. "Google supercharges machine learning tasks with TPU custom chip." (2016) *https://cloudplatform.googleblog.com/2016/05/Google-supercharges-machine-learning-tasks-with-custom-chip.html*.

3. *https://www.tensorflow.org/* and "Chapter 3. The Java HotSpot Compilers." *http://www.oracle.com/technetwork/java/whitepaper-135217.html#compover*.

4. "Amazon Machine Images (AMI)." *http://amzn.to/2vapEL1*.

5. "AMI Types." *http://amzn.to/2ivjv6a*.

6. "Instance Lifecycle." *http://amzn.to/1Fw5S8l*.

7. "AMI Creation with Aminator." (2013) *http://techblog.netflix.com/2013/03/ami-creation-with-aminator.html*.

8. "Deploying the Netflix API." (2013) *http://techblog.netflix.com/2013/08/deploying-netflix-api.html*.

9. *Continuous Delivery* (2010) *https://martinfowler.com/books/continuousDelivery.html*.

10. "Global Continuous Delivery with Spinnaker." (2015) *http://techblog.netflix.com/2015/11/global-continuous-delivery-with.html*.

CHAPTER SIX

Autoscaling

In Chapter 5, we talked about installing hardware in your on-premises datacenter and its deployment to production. As it is well known, use of public cloud obviates the need for this. Further, it obviates the need for maintenance of the infrastructure and thereby boosts product development agility, which is crucial in an increasingly competitive landscape. For instance, in 2008, Netflix kicked off its migration from on-premises to Amazon Web Services (AWS), and in February 2016, it announced the completion of the migration of its streaming service to the cloud.[1] Migration to the cloud eliminated the cycles spent on hardware procurement and datacenter maintenance, and resulted in higher development agility.

The use of a cloud service at large scale is much more expensive compared to the use of an in-house datacenter. This calls for the development of techniques to minimize the cost overhead associated with the use of a public cloud without sacrificing its various benefits such as elasticity. Autoscaling allows automatic scaling up of capacity when it is needed and scaling back down when it is not needed. An enterprise can set a minimum required capacity across *Availability Zones* (AZs)—isolated locations in a given geographic region—to ensure quick accessibility. This helps save cost by providing the best availability and performance for a given cost. For cases in which a reserved capacity is purchased, the cost can be amortized by scheduling jobs of non-critical and batch services during the off-peak hours.

NOTE

This part of the discussion is based in Arun's experience at Netflix.

---

1 "Completing the Netflix Cloud Migration." (2016) *https://media.netflix.com/en/company-blog/completing-the-netflix-cloud-migration*

The Challenge

Capitalizing on the elasticity of the cloud efficiently is nontrivial. Specifically, you must be wary of the following:

- Aggressive scale-down can potentially adversely affect latency and throughput (in the worst case, the service might become unavailable). Higher latency would degrade the experience of the end users. Further, from a corporate standpoint, lower throughput would adversely impact the bottom line (this holds in general for any end-user facing service).

- Aggressive scale-up can result in overprovisioning, thereby ballooning the footprint on the cloud. Of course, higher operational costs would adversely affect the bottom line.

Figure 6-1 illustrates these caveats. Additionally, efficient exploitation of elasticity of the cloud across multiple applications can contain the overall footprint.

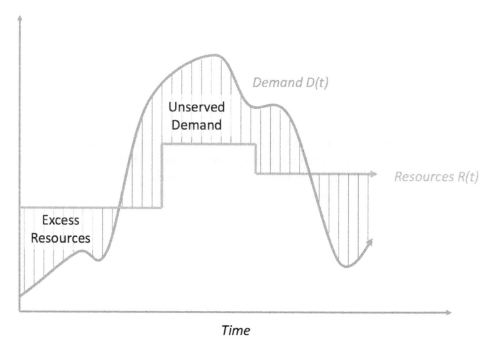

Figure 6-1. *Excess versus unserved demand*

In the long run, on-demand usage is much more expensive than the use of reserved instances.[2] Consequently, it is critical to develop novel techniques to exploit elasticity of the cloud systematically.

Spot Market in Public Clouds

For most public clouds, you can bid for unused instances. These instances are priced up to 90 percent lower than On-Demand instance and thereby can lower your costs significantly. On Amazon EC2, such instances are referred to as *Spot instances*.[3] A spot market is a market where standardized products are traded for immediate delivery. The price of the products on the market depends on supply and demand. Google Compute Engine's Preemptible Virtual Machines are the equivalent of Amazon EC2 Spot instances. In the interest of brevity, in this sidebar we discuss only the various key aspects related to Amazon EC2 Spot instances.

The hourly price for a Spot instance (of each instance type in each Availability Zone) is set by Amazon EC2, and fluctuates depending on the supply of and demand for Spot instances. A Spot instance runs whenever the bid exceeds the current market price. When the current Spot price rises above your bid price, the Spot instance is reclaimed by AWS. A two-minute warning, formally known as a Spot Instance Termination Notice, is made available when an instance has been marked for termination so that the application can use this time to save its state, upload final logfiles, or remove itself from an Elastic Load Balancer (ELB). To allow in-flight requests to complete when de-registering Spot instances that are about to be terminated, you can enable *connection draining* on the load balancer with a timeout of 90 seconds. Connection draining causes the ELB load balancer to stop sending new requests to a de-registering instance or an unhealthy instance, while keeping the existing connections open.

Spot instances are a cost-effective choice if there's flexibility with respect to when an application is run and whether the application can potentially be interrupted. For example, Spot instances are well-suited for Monte-Carlo simulations, video transcoding, batch jobs, background processing, and so on. Further, it's critical that you ensure that the application can start running on Spot instances quickly.[4]

You can create a Lambda function to dynamically manage Auto Scaling Groups (ASGs) based on the Spot market. The Lambda function could periodically invoke the EC2 Spot APIs to assess market prices and availability and respond by creating new

---

2 We encourage you to compare the prices of Reserved and On-Demand instances on AWS at *https://aws.amazon.com/ec2/pricing/*.

3 For further information about Spot instances, go to *http://docs.aws.amazon.com/AWSEC2/latest/UserGuide/using-spot-instances.html*.

4 As per Mike Tung of Diffbot, bidding, allocation, and booting of Spot instances at Amazon's end is quite fast—in the neighborhood of two to three minutes. Configuring the instance and loading the job is typically the bottleneck. The bottleneck is supposedly worse with Spot instances than with on-demand instances. For further details, go to *http://blog.diffbot.com/setting-up-a-machine-learning-farm-in-the-cloud-with-spot-instances-auto-scaling/*.

autoscaling launch configurations and groups automatically. Likewise, the Lambda function could also delete any Spot ASGs and launch configurations that have no instances.

A spot market is defined by the following:

- Instance type
- Region
- AZ

Each spot market offers its own current price. In light of this, you should try to use different instance types in different AZs (or even regions) because it allows you to pick the
lowest price available. Figure 6-2 (borrowed from "Revenue Maximization for Cloud
Computing Services," by C. Kilcioglu and C. Maglaras, 2015) illustrates the variation of
Spot price by instance type. A recent research argues that prices of Spot instances are
usually not market-driven as sometimes previously assumed (see "Deconstructing Amazon EC2 Spot Instance Pricing," by O. A. Ben-Yehuda et al. 2013.); on the contrary, the
prices of Spot instances are typically generated at random from within a tight price
interval via a dynamic hidden reserve price. For more information on how to bid for Spot
instances in the cloud, go to "Readings" on page 180.

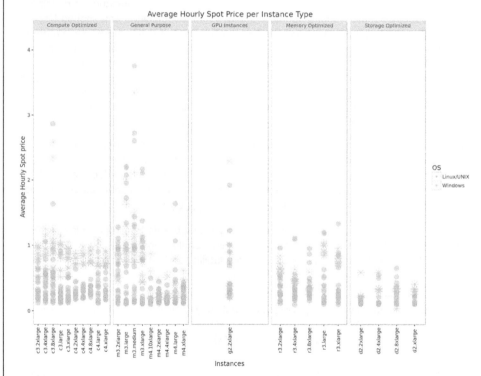

Figure 6-2. Spot Price_by Instance Type

In May 2015, AWS announced the Spot Fleet—a fleet is a collection of Spot instances
that are all working together as part of a distributed application—API that makes it possi-

ble for you to launch and manage an entire fleet of Spot instances with one request. This obviated the need to write custom code for discovering capacity, monitoring market prices across instance types and availability zones, and managing bids. Having said that, a Spot Fleet is not fault-tolerant and hence can experience availability and performance degradation induced by sudden termination of Spot instances. One strategy to address this is to launch a core group of On-Demand instances[5] to maintain a minimum level of guaranteed compute resources and supplement them with Spot instances when the opportunity arises. Figure 6-3 illustrates this concept.

Provisioning for different fault-tolerant levels using 2 or more spot types

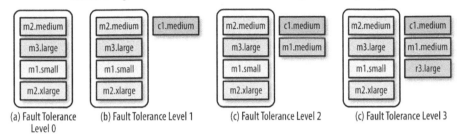

(a) Fault Tolerance Level 0   (b) Fault Tolerance Level 1   (c) Fault Tolerance Level 2   (c) Fault Tolerance Level 3

Provisioning for different fault-tolerant levels using mixture of on-demand and spot instances

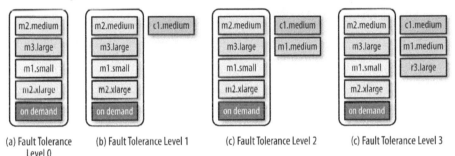

(a) Fault Tolerance Level 0   (b) Fault Tolerance Level 1   (c) Fault Tolerance Level 2   (c) Fault Tolerance Level 3

Figure 6-3. (a) Provisioning for different fault-tolerant levels using 2 more spot types (b) Provisioning for different fault-tolerant levels using a mixture of On-Demand and Spot instances

You can place ASGs running On-Demand instances together with ASGs running Spot instances using different Spot bid prices behind the same ELB. This provides more flexibility and helps to meet changing traffic demands. Another strategy is to launch Spot

---

5 The key differences between Spot instances and On-Demand instances are that Spot instances might not start immediately, the hourly price for Spot instances varies based on demand, and Amazon EC2 can terminate an individual Spot instance as the hourly price for or availability of Spot instances changes.

instances with a required duration (also known as *Spot blocks*), which are not interrupted due to changes in the Spot price.

It's not uncommon that a margin on each instance is kept to handle short-term workload surge and thereby provide a buffer to buy time for booting up new instances. This margin empirically ranges from 20 to 25 percent of the instance's capacity. With over-provisioning (as illustrated in Figure 6-3), this margin can be reduced when using Spot instances. The margin can change dynamically based on the current fault-tolerant level. Because higher a fault-tolerant level results in a greater amount of overprovisioning, you can be more aggressive in reducing the margin of each instance.

Akin to the Spot instances on AWS, Google Preemptible VMs may be shut down at any time and are well suited for distributed, fault-tolerant workloads that do not require continuous availability of any single instance. When Preemptible VMs are terminated, they receive a 30-second notice–this is in contrast to the two-minute notice in case of Spot instances on AWS–giving you the opportunity to shut down cleanly (including saving work, if applicable). For more information about Preemptible VMs, go to *https:// cloud.google.com/compute/docs/instances/preemptible*.

For the remainder of this chapter, we discuss the various aspects of autoscaling using Amazon EC2 as a reference public cloud. The key underlying concepts are, however, applicable for autoscaling on any public cloud.

Autoscaling on Amazon EC2

Amazon's Auto Scaling service lets you launch or terminate EC2 instances (up to a defined minimum and maximum, respectively) automatically based on user-defined policies, schedules, and health checks. You can use Amazon's CloudWatch for real-time monitoring of EC2 instances. Metrics such as CPU utilization, latency, and request counts are provided automatically by CloudWatch. Further, you can use CloudWatch to access up-to-the-minute statistics, view graphs, and set *alarms* (defined here):

Definition 1

An Amazon CloudWatch *alarm* is an object that watches over a single metric. An alarm can change state depending on the value of the metric. An action is invoked when an alarm changes state and remains in that state for a number of time periods.

You can configure a CloudWatch alarm to send a message to autoscaling whenever a specific metric has reached a threshold value. When the alarm sends the message, autoscaling executes the associated *policy* on an ASG to scale the group up or down. Note that an Auto Scaling action is invoked when the specified metric remains above the threshold value for a number of time periods. This is to ensure that a scaling action is not triggered due to a sudden spike in the metric.

Definition 2

A *policy* is a set of instructions for Auto Scaling that instructs the service how to respond to CloudWatch alarm messages.

Separate policies are instituted for autoscaling up and autoscaling down. The two key parameters associated with an Auto Scaling Policy are the following:

- `ScalingAdjustment`: The number of instances by which to scale. `AdjustmentType` determines the interpretation of this number (e.g., as an absolute number or as a percentage of the existing ASG size). A positive increment adds to the current capacity and a negative value removes from the current capacity.

- `AdjustmentType`: This specifies whether the `ScalingAdjustment` is an absolute number or a percentage of the current capacity. Valid values are `ChangeIn Capacity` or `PercentChangeInCapacity` (described later in the chapter).

An autoscaling action, say scale up, usually takes a while to take effect. In light of this, you can specify a *cooldown* period (defined momentarily) to ensure that a new autoscaling event is triggered after the completion of the previous autoscaling event.

Definition 3

Cooldown is the period of time after autoscaling initiates a scaling activity during which no other scaling activity can take place. A cooldown period allows the effect of a scaling activity to become visible in the metrics that originally triggered the activity. This period is configurable and gives the system time to perform and adjust to any new scaling activities (such as scale-in and scale-out) that affect capacity.

On AWS, autoscaling also can be carried in a temporal fashion, referred to as *scheduled scaling*. In particular, scaling based on a schedule allows you to scale an application in response to predictable load changes. For instance, if the traffic begins to increase on Friday evening and remains high until Sunday evening, you can scale activities based on the predictable traffic patterns of the web application. To create a scheduled scaling action, you must specify the start time of the scaling action and the new minimum, maximum, and desired sizes for the scaling action. At the specified time, autoscaling updates the group with the values for minimum, maximum, and desired size specified by the scaling action.

At Netflix, we employed *scaling by policy* wherein a given cluster was scaled up/down based on the incoming request per second (RPS) of a given application. We used incoming RPS as the metric to drive autoscaling because it is independent of the application and directly relates to throughput.

Design Guidelines

In this section, we detail the various design guidelines underlying the algorithms for autoscaling discussed later in this chapter.

Avoiding the ping-pong effect

During a scale up event, new nodes are added to a given ASG. As a consequence, the RPS per node drops. However, if the RPS per node drops below the threshold specified for scaling down an ASG, it would trigger a scale-down event. This would result in alternating scale-up and scale-down events, as illustrated in Figure 6-4 (a), and referred to as a *ping-pong effect*. At Netflix, we observed that ping-ponging can potentially result in higher latency and, in the worst case, can cause violation of the Service-Level Agreement (SLA) of the service.

Thus, when defining the autoscaling policies, it is imperative to ensure that the policy is not susceptible to ping-pong effect. The desired autoscaling profile is exemplified by Figure 6-4 (b).

(a)   (b)

Figure 6-4. *(a) Illustrating ping-pong effect (b) Desired autoscaling profile (Y-axis corresponds to the number of nodes in the ASG and X-axis corresponds to time)*

Be proactive, not reactive

As mentioned earlier, applications such as the recommendation engine at Netflix take a long time to start. This can be ascribed to a variety of reasons; for example, loading of metadata of Netflix subscribers and precomputation of certain features. For such applications, it is critical to trigger the scale-up event in a proactive fashion, not reactively.

Let us consider the scenario shown in Figure 6-5. The solid arrow in the figure corresponds to the need to scale-up a given ASG as mandated by the SLA and increasing traffic. However, owing to a long application startup time, the autoscaling up is triggered, signified by the dashed arrow in the figure, proactively. The proactive approach ensures that the ASG is sufficiently provisioned by the time the latency approaches the SLA and that the SLA is never violated!

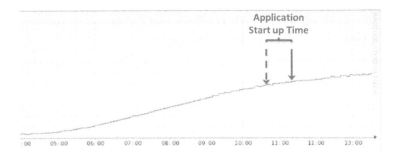

Figure 6-5. *Illustration of scaling in a proactive fashion. Solid arrow signifies the need to scale up (as governed by SLA of the application at hand) and the dashed arrow signifies the corresponding autoscaling event (governed by the start up of the application)*

Aggressive upwards, conservative downwards

Delivering the best user experience is critical for business. Thus, you might want to employ an aggressive scale-up policy so as to be able to handle a more-than-expected increase in traffic. Also, an aggressive scale-up approach provides a buffer for increase in traffic during the cooldown period. In contrast, you might want to employ a conservative scale-down policy so as to be able to handle a slower (than the historical trend) ramp-down of traffic. Aggressive scale-down might accidentally result in under-provisioning, thereby adversely affecting latency and throughout.

Scalability Analysis

Determining the threshold for scale-up is an integral step is defining an autoscaling policy. A low threshold will result in under-utilization of the instances in the ASG; conversely, a high threshold can result in higher latency, thereby degrading the user experience. To this end, load testing is carried out to determine the throughput corresponding to the SLA of application (see Figure 6-6).

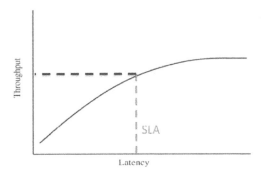

Figure 6-6. *Trade-off between latency and throughput (load)*

Properties

Each scale-up event should satisfy the following:

Property 1
 RPS per node after scale up should be more than the scale-down threshold (T_D).

Property 1 ensures that scale-up does not induce a ping-pong effect. Likewise, each scale-down event should satisfy the following:

Property 2
 RPS per node after scale-down should be less than the scale-up threshold (T_U).

Akin to Property 1, Property 2 also ensures that scale-up does not induce a ping-pong effect.

Autoscaling by Fixed Amount

In this section, we present a technique for scaling an ASG up/down by a fixed number of instances and as per the guidelines laid out earlier. `AdjustmentType` for the scaling policy is set to `ChangeInCapacity`, which is defined as follows:

`ChangeInCapacity`
 This `AdjustmentType` is used to increase or decrease the capacity by a fixed amount on top of the existing capacity. For instance, let's assume that the capacity of a given ASG is three and that `ChangeInCapacity` is set to five. When the policy is executed, autoscaling will add five more instances to ASG.

Algorithm 1 (shown in the following section) details the parameters and the steps to determine the scaling thresholds (for both scaling up and scaling down). The scale-down value D and the scale-up value U are inputs to the algorithm. The constants 0.90 and 0.50 used in defining T_U, T_D were determined empirically so as to minimize the impact on user experience and contain ASG under-utilization. Loop L1 in Algorithm 1 corresponds to scaling up an ASG as the incoming traffic increases. Loop L2 in Algorithm 1 scales down an ASG as the incoming traffic decreases.

Algorithm 1—autoscaling up/down by a fixed amount

Input
 An application with a specified SLA.

Parameters
 D Scale down value

 U Scale up value

 T_D Scale down threshold (RPS per node)

T_U Scale up threshold (RPS per node)

$N_{\min}$ Minimum number of nodes in the ASG

Let T (SLA) return the maximum RPS per node for the specified SLA.

$T_U \leftarrow 0.90 \times T$ (SLA)

$T_D \leftarrow 0.50 \times T_U$

Let N_c, RPS_n denote the current number of nodes and RPS per node respectively

L1: /* Scale Up (if $RPS_n > T_U$ */

repeat

$N_{(c_{old})} \leftarrow N_c$

$N_c \leftarrow N_c + U$

$RPS_n \leftarrow RPS_n * N_{(c_{old})} / N_c$

until $RPS_n > T_U$

L2: /* Scale Down (if $RPS_n < T_D$) */

repeat

$N_{(c_{old})} \leftarrow N_c$

$N_c \leftarrow max(N_{\min}, N_c - D)$

$RPS_n \leftarrow RPS_n * N_{(c_{old})} / N_c$

until $RPS_n < T_D$ or $N_c = N_{\min}$

Illustration of Algorithm 1

For a better understanding of Algorithm 1, let's walk through a case study. The parameters of the algorithm are listed before Tables 6-1 and 6-2. Initially, $RPS_{ASG} = 500$ and $N_c = 6$. As RPS_{ASG} increases to 1540, RPS_n approaches T_U. An autoscaling up-event is triggered thereby adding 3 (= U) nodes to the ASG. As RPS_{ASG} increases subsequently, autoscaling up-events are triggered. Note that all the entries in column six satisfy Property 1.

During scale-down, the initial $RPS_{ASG} = 5000$ and $N_c = 18$. As RPS_{ASG} decreases to 3240, and RPS_n approaches T_D. An autoscaling down-event is triggered, thereby deleting 2 (= D) nodes from the ASG. Note that all the entries in column 12 satisfy Property 2.

Illustration of Algorithm 1 (D =2, U = 3, T_D = 180, T_U = 230)

Table 6-1. *Scale Up*

# Nodes (current)	Nodes added	RPS_{ASG}	RPS_n	Total nodes	New RPS_n
6	0	500	83.33	6	
		1740			
	3			9	193.33
		2610			
	3			12	217.50
		3480			
	3			15	232.00
		4350			
	3			18	241.67
		5520			
	3			21	248.57

Table 6-2. *Scale Down*

# Nodes (current)	Nodes added	RPS_{ASG}	RPS_n	Total nodes	New RPS_n
18		5000	277.78	18	
		3240			
	2			16	202.50
		2880			
	2			14	205.71
		2520			
	2			12	210.00
		2160			
	2			10	216.00
		1800			
	2			8	225.00

Scaling by Percentage

In this section, we present a technique for scaling an ASG up or down by a percentage of current capacity and as per the guidelines laid out earlier. AdjustmentType for the scaling policy is set to PercentChangeInCapacity, which is defined here:

PercentChangeInCapacity

> This AdjustmentType is used to increase or decrease the capacity by a percentage of the desired capacity. For instance, let's assume that an ASG has 15 instances and a scaling-up policy of the type PercentChangeInCapacity and adjustment set to 15. When the policy is run, autoscaling will increase the ASG size by two.

> Note that if the PercentChangeInCapacity returns a value between 0 and 1, autoscaling will round it off to 1. If the PercentChangeInCapacity returns a value greater than 1, autoscaling will round it off to the lower value.

Algorithm 2 details the parameters and the steps to determine the scaling thresholds (for both scaling up and scaling down). The scale-down value D and the scale-up value U (note that both are percentages) are inputs to the algorithm. The constants 0.90 and 0.50 used in defining T_U and T_D were determined empirically so as to minimize impact on user experience and contain ASG under utilization. Loop L1 in Algorithm 2 corresponds to scaling up an ASG as the incoming traffic increases. Loop L2 in Algorithm 2 scales down an ASG as the incoming traffic decreases.

Algorithm 2—autoscaling up/down by a percentage of current capacity

Input
> An application with a specified SLA.

Parameters
> D Scale down percentage value

> U Scale up percentage value

> T_D Scale down threshold (RPS per node)

> T_U Scale up threshold (RPS per node)

> N_{min} Minimum number of nodes in the ASG

Let T (SLA) return the maximum RPS per node for the specified SLA.

$T_U \leftarrow 0.90 \times T \text{ (SLA)}$

$T_D \leftarrow 0.50 \times T_U$

Let N_c, RPS_n denote the current number of nodes and RPS per node respectively

L1: /* Scale Up (if $RPS_n > T_U$) */

repeat

$$N_{(c_{old})} \leftarrow N_c$$

$$N_c \leftarrow N_c + \max(1, N_c \times U/100)$$

$$RPS_n \leftarrow RPS_n * N_{(c_{old})}/N_c$$

until $RPS_n > T_U$

L2: /* Scale Down (if $RPS_n < T_D$ */

repeat

$$N_{(c_{old})} \leftarrow N_c$$

$$N_c \leftarrow \max(N_{min}, N_c - \max(1, N_c \times D/100))$$

$$RPS_n \leftarrow RPS_n * N_{(c_{old})}/N_c$$

until $RPS_n < T_D$ or $N_c = N_{min}$

Illustration of Algorithm 2

For a better understanding of Algorithm 2, let's again walk through a case study. The parameters of the algorithm are mentioned before Tables 6-3 and 6-4. N_{min} is set to 1. Initially, $RPS_{ASG} = 500$ and $N_c = 6$. As RPS_{ASG} increases to 1540 and RPS_n approaches T_U, an autoscaling up-event is triggered, thereby adding 1 (= max(1, 6 × 10/100) node to the ASG. As RPS_{ASG} increases subsequently, autoscaling up-events are triggered. Note that all the entries in column six satisfy Property 1.

During scale-down, the initial $RPS_{ASG} = 5000$ and $N_c = 18$. As RPS_{ASG} decreases to 4140, RPS_n approaches T_D. An autoscaling down-event is triggered thereby deleting 1 (= max(1, .18 * 8/100.)) node from the ASG. Note that all the entries in column 12 satisfy Property 2.

Illustration of Algorithm 2 ($D = 8$, $U = 10$, $N_{min} = 1$, $T_D = 230$, $T_U = 290$)

Table 6-3. *Scale Up*

# Nodes (current)	Nodes added	RPS_{ASG}	RPS_n	Total nodes	New RPS_n
6	0	500	83.33	6	
		1740			
	1			7	248.57
		2030			
	1			8	253.75
		2320			
	1			9	257.78
		2610			
	1			10	261.00
		2900			
	1			11	263.64
		3190			
	1			12	265.83
		3480			
	1			13	267.69
		3770			
	1			14	269.29
		4060			
	1			15	270.67
		4350			
	1			16	271.88
		4640			
	1			17	272.94
		4930			
	1			18	273.89
		5220			
	1			19	274.74

Table 6-4. *Scale Down*

# Nodes (current)	Nodes added	RPS$_{ASG}$	RPS$_n$	Total nodes	New RPS$_n$
18		5000	277.78	18	
		4140			
	1			17	243.53
		3910			
	1			16	244.38
		3680			
	1			15	245.33
		3450			
	1			14	246.43
		3220			
	1			13	247.69
		2990			
	1			12	249.17
		2760			
	1			11	250.91
		2530			
	1			10	253.00
		2300			
	1			9	255.56
		2070			
	1			8	258.75
		1840			
	1			7	262.86
		1610			
	1			6	268.33

Upon comparing the illustrations of Algorithms 1 and 2, we note that the threshold values U and D are higher in the case of the latter. This boosts hardware utilization and reduces the footprint on the cloud.

Startup Time Aware Scaling

In this section, we extend Algorithm 2 to guide autoscaling for applications with long startup times. Long application startup times can be ascribed to a variety of reasons; for example, loading of metadata. As discussed earlier, in the presence of long startup times, autoscaling up needs to be done proactively. For this, we employ the following steps:

- For a historical time–series of RPS in production, determine the change in RPS over every A_{start} minutes, where A_{start} denotes the application startup time. This would yield a time–series with these data points:

  $RPS_{Astart} - RPS_0$

  $RPS_{Astart+1} - RPS_1$

  $RPS_{Astart+2} - RPS_2$

  $RPS_{Astart+3} - RPS_3$

  .

  .

  .

  where RPS_t denotes the RPS at time t. The derived time–series, referred to as rolling RPS change, captures the change in RPS in any window of width A_{start} minutes.

- Compute the 99th percentile of the rolling time–series, denoted by R_RPS.

- Compute $\gamma = T_U - R_{RPS}$. The parameter γ is the effective threshold for scale up. The use of 99th percentile of the rolling RPS change time–series is consistent with the Aggressive Upwards guideline outlined earlier.

The top of Figure 6-7 shows an example RPS time–series (with one-minute granularity) of an application. The startup time of the application was 30 minutes. The corresponding rolling RPS time–series is shown at the bottom of Figure 6-7. The 99th percentile of the rolling time–series is 1.109.

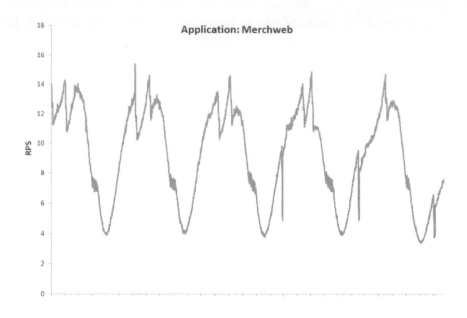

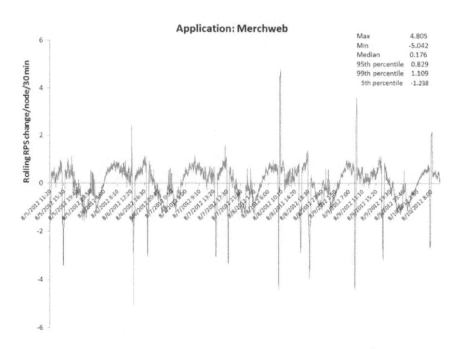

Figure 6-7. *Rolling change in RPS_n for an application startup time of 30 minutes*

Algorithm 3 details the parameters and the steps to determine the scaling thresholds (for both scaling up and scaling down). The scale-down value D and the scale-up value U are inputs to the algorithm. The constants 0.90 and 0.50 used in defining T_U, T_D were determined empirically so as to minimize the impact on user experience and contain ASG under-utilization. Loop L1 in "Algorithm 3" corresponds to scaling-up an ASG as the incoming traffic increases. Loop L2 in Algorithm 3 scales-down an ASG as the incoming traffic decreases. Unlike scale-up, the threshold for scale-down D need not be adjusted, because applications do not induce a long delay during termination of instances on Amazon's EC2.

Algorithm 3—application start up aware autoscaling up/down by a percentage of current capacity

Input
    An application with a specified SLA.

Parameters
    D Scale down percentage value

    U Scale up percentage value

    A_{start} Application start up time (mins)

    T_D Scale down threshold (RPS per node)

    T_U Scale up threshold (RPS per node)

    N_{min} Minimum number of nodes in the ASG

Let T(SLA) return the maximum RPS per node for the specified SLA.

$T_U \leftarrow 0.90 \times T(\text{SLA})$

$T_D \leftarrow 0.50 \times T_U$

Let N_c, RPS_n denote the current number of nodes and RPS per node respectively

Transform RPS time series to a rolling A_{start} (min) time series

Let R_{RPS} denote the 99th percentile of the rolling time series

Let $\gamma = T_U - R_{\text{RPS}}$

L1: /* Scale Up (if $\text{RPS}_n > \gamma$) */

repeat

$$N_{(c_{old})} \leftarrow N_c$$

$$N_c \leftarrow N_c + \max(1, N_c \times U/100)$$

$$\text{RPS}_n \leftarrow \text{RPS}_n * N_{(c_{old})}/N_c$$

until $\text{RPS}_n > T_U$

L2: /* Scale Down (if $\text{RPS}_n < T_D$) */

repeat

$$N_{(c_{old})} \leftarrow N_c$$

$$N_c \leftarrow \max(N_{\min}, N_c - \max(1, N_c \times D/100))$$

$$\text{RPS}_n \leftarrow \text{RPS}_n * N_{(c_{old})}/N_c$$

until $\text{RPS}_n < T_D$ or $N_c = N_{\min}$

Illustration of Algorithm 3

For a better understanding of Algorithm 3, let's one more time walk through a case study (refer to Tables 6-5 and 6-6). The RPS and the rolling RPS change time–series for the application are shown in Figure 6-7, respectively. The parameters of the algorithm are mentioned before Tables 6-5 and 6-6. $N_{\min}$ is set to 1. Initially, $\text{RPS}_{\text{ASG}} = 800$, $N_c = 170$, and $\gamma = 12.9$. As RPS_{ASG} increases to 2193, RPS_n approaches γ. An autoscaling up-event is triggered, thereby adding 25 (= $\max(1, 170 \times 15/100)$) nodes to the ASG. As RPS_{ASG} increases subsequently, autoscaling up-events are triggered. Note that all the entries in column seven satisfy Property 1.

During scale down, the initial $\text{RPS}_{\text{ASG}} = 4400$ and $N_c = 389$. As RPS_{ASG} decreases to 3890, RPS_n approaches T_D. An autoscaling down-event gets triggered thereby deleting 38 (= $\max(1, 389 \times 10/100)$) nodes from the ASG. Note that all the entries in column 13 satisfy Property 2.

Illustration of Algorithm 3 ($D = 10$, $U = 15$, $U_{min} = 1$, $A_{START} = 30$, $R_{RPS} = 1.1$, $T_D = 10$, $T_U = 14$)

Table 6-5. *Scale Up*

# Nodes (current)	Nodes added	RPS$_{ASG}$	RPS$_n$	$\gamma = T_U - R_{RPS}$	Total nodes	New RPS$_n$
170	0	800	4.71	12.9	170	
		2193				
	25				195	11.25
		2515.5				
	29				224	11.23
		2889.6				
	33				257	11.24
		3315.3				
	38				295	11.24
		3805.5				
	44				339	11.23
		4373.1				
	50				389	11.24
		5018.1				

Table 6-6. *Scale Down*

# Nodes (current)	Nodes added	RPS$_{ASG}$	RPS$_n$	Total nodes	New RPS$_n$
389		4400	11.31	389	
		3890			
	38			351	11.08
		3510			
	35			316	11.11
		3160			
	31			285	11.09
		2850			
	28			257	11.09
		2570			
	25			232	11.08
		2320			
	23			209	11.10
		2090			

Potpourri

There have been cases wherein the CPU utilization on production nodes spiked without any increase in traffic. This can happen to a variety of accidental events. To handle such cases, instituting add-on scale-up policies (i.e., besides a scale-up policy based on RPS), as exemplified in Figure 6-8, helps to mitigate the impact on the end users.

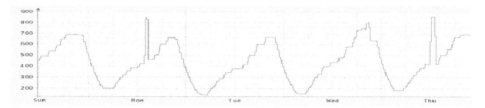

Figure 6-8. *Add-on policies to check "meltdown"*

In July 2015, AWS introduced new scaling policies with steps. For example, you can specify different responses for different levels of average CPU utilization, say <50%, [50%, 60%), [60%, 80%), and ≥80%. Further, if you create multiple-step scaling policies for the same resource (perhaps based on CPU utilization and inbound network traffic) and both of them fire at approximately the same time, autoscaling will look at both policies and choose the one that results in the change of the highest magnitude.

> ——— NOTE ———
> For further information, go to *https://aws.amazon.com/blogs/aws/auto-scaling-update-new-scaling-policies-for-more-responsive-scaling/*.

In certain scenarios, you might want to protect certain instances in an ASG from termination. For example, an instance might be handling a long-running work task, perhaps pulled from an SQS queue. Protecting the instance from termination will avoid wasted work. In a similar vein, an instance might serve a special purpose within the group; for example, it could be the master node of a Hadoop cluster, or a "canary" that flags the entire group of instances as up and running. To this end, you can use the Instance Protection Feature offered by AWS. In most cases, at least one instance in an ASG should be left unprotected; if all of the instances are protected, no scale action will be taken.

> ——— NOTE ———
> For further information, go to *https://aws.amazon.com/blogs/aws/new-instance-protection-for-auto-scaling/*.

Leading companies such as Netflix and Facebook have been using autoscaling to improve cluster performance, service availability, and reduce costs. In its post, Facebook shared the following:

> ...a particular type of web server at Facebook consumes about 60 watts of power when it's idle (0 RPS, or requests-per-second). The power consumption jumps to 130 watts when it runs at low-level CPU utilization (small RPS). But when it runs at medium-level CPU utilization, power consumption increases only slightly to 150 watts. Therefore, from a power-efficiency perspective, we should try to avoid running a server at low RPS and instead try to run at medium RPS.

For details, refer to the following:

- *http://techblog.netflix.com/2013/12/scryer-netflixs-predictive-auto-scaling.html*
- *http://bit.ly/fb-infrastructure-autoscale*

Besides RPS, other metrics have been used for autoscaling: CPU utilization, memory usage, disk I/O bandwidth, network link load, peak workload, jobs in progress, service rate, the number of concurrent users, the number of active connections, jitter, delay, and the average response time per request. Regression modeling has been employed for predicting the amount of resources needed for the actual workload and possibly retract over-provisioned resources. Likewise, several other approaches have been employed for resource-demand prediction such as prediction based on changes in the request arrival rate (i.e., the slope of the workload). You can employ sensitivity analysis to characterize the different types of inputs and determine the types of resources that have the highest impact on the throughput (or the performance metric of interest) of the application. Subsequently, you can set up multiple autoscaling rules based on one or more resource types.

In recent years, the use of containers has received wide attention. Amazon EC2 Container Service (ECS), Google Container Engine, and Microsoft Azure Container Service are the most popular public container services. Multi-AZ clusters make the ECS infrastructure highly available, thereby providing a safeguard from potential zone failure. The AZ–aware ECS scheduler manages, scales, and distributes the tasks across the cluster, thus making the architecture highly available. On AWS, akin to the EC2 instances, autoscaling policies also can be defined for ECS instances. You can use the approaches discussed earlier in this chapter in the context of autoscaling container instances, as well.

Advanced Approaches

Given the importance of exploiting the elasticity of the cloud in the best possible fashion, several advanced techniques have been proposed for autoscaling in both the industry and the academia. For instance, Facebook employed the classic control theory and proportional-integral (PI) controller to achieve fast reaction time. Netflix developed two prediction algorithms—one of which is an augmented linear regression–based algorithm, the other based on Fast Fourier Transform (FFT). One of the key highlights of the Netflix approach is that it's predictive. Specifically, its approach learns the request pattern based on historical data and subsequently drives the scale-up or scale-down action. Both approaches have been deployed in production environments. Given that no comparative analysis was presented, it is difficult to assess how these techniques fare against the techniques that were proposed previously.

Many other approaches for autoscaling have been proposed based on control theory, queuing theory, fuzzy logic, neural networks, reinforcement learning, support vector machines, wavelet transform, regression splines, pattern matching, Kalman filters, sliding window, proportional thresholding, second-order regression, histograms, time–series models, the secant method, voting system, and look-ahead control. In most cases, these techniques "learn" from past traffic patterns and resource usage and hence are unable to adapt with any new pattern that might appear as a result of the dynamic nature of the web traffic.

NOTE

For more information, refer to the section "Readings" on page 180.

In practice, applicability of autoscaling approaches based on the preceding is limited owing to a wide variety of reasons. For instance, reinforcement learning–based approaches require a long time to learn and adapt only to slowly changing conditions. Therefore, you cannot apply such techniques to real applications that usually experience sudden traffic bursts. In a similar vein, queuing theory–based approaches impose hard assumptions that are typically not valid for real, complex systems. Besides, such approaches are intended for stationary scenarios and hence you will need to recalculate the queuing model when the conditions of the application change. In the case of control theory–based approaches, determining the gain parameters is nontrivial.

Summary

At times, we observe spikes in incoming traffic. This can happen due to a variety reasons. For instance, at the end of events such as the Super Bowl, you would observe (as expected) a sudden rise in incoming traffic (e.g., number of tweets). Figure 6-9 presents an example traffic profile with spikes. State-of-the-art autoscaling techniques do not fare well against such spikes.

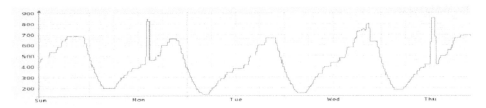

Figure 6-9. *Spikes in load in production*

Akin to the preceding, "burstiness" in the workload at finer timescales (in the order of seconds) can potentially adversely affect the efficacy of autoscaling techniques, as demonstrated in Figure 6-10.

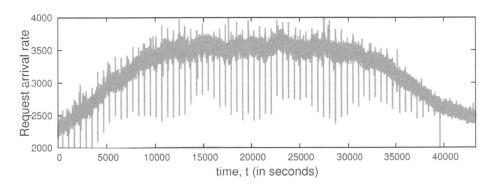

Figure 6-10. *A bursty workload*

In the under-provisioning scenario, fine-scale burstiness can potentially cause an increased queuing effect and a high request defection rate, thereby resulting in increased SLA violations. On the other hand, in the over-provisioning scenario, fine-scale burstiness can potentially result in reduced resource utilization at the application server. Thus, as a community, we need to build support for fine-grained monitoring and develop more agile, adaptive policies to guarantee effective elasticity under fine-scale burstiness.

Autoscaling a service down independent of the traffic upstream can potentially result in meltdowns. Thus, it is critical to develop autoscaling techniques that capture the interaction between different services in a Service-Oriented Architecture (SOA). Outages in the cloud and in datacenters (see "Resources" on page 182) have been becoming increasingly more frequent. One of the ways to minimize the impact of outages is to extend the SOA to span multiple Infrastructure as a Service (IaaS) vendors. This would in turn call for extending the techniques proposed in this chapter to be vendor-aware.

Readings

1. *http://docs.rightscale.com/cm/dashboard/manage/arrays/arrays_actions.html#set-up-autoscaling-using-voting-tags*

2. A. Ilyushkin et al. (2017). *An Experimental Performance Evaluation of Autoscaling Policies for Complex Workflows.*

3. A. V. Papadopoulos et al. (2016). *PEAS: A Performance Evaluation Framework for Auto-Scaling Strategies in Cloud Applications.*

4. M. Grechanik et al. (2016). *Enhancing Rules For Cloud Resource Provisioning Via Learned Software Performance Models.*

5. C. Qu et al. (2016). *A reliable and cost-efficient auto-scaling system for web applications using heterogeneous spot instances.*

6. L. Zheng et al. (2015). *How to Bid the Cloud.*

7. A. N. Toosi et al. (2015). *SipaaS: Spot instance pricing as a Service framework and its implementation in OpenStack.*

8. W. Guo et al. (2015). *Bidding for Highly Available Services with Low Price in Spot Instance Market.*

9. S. Islam et al. (2015). *Evaluating the impact of fine-scale burstiness on cloud elasticity.*

10. V. R. Messias et al. (2015). *Combining time series prediction models using genetic algorithm to autoscaling Web applications hosted in the cloud infrastructure.*

11. M. Beltran. (2015). *Defining an Elasticity Metric for Cloud Computing Environments.*

12. A. Y. Nikravesh et al. (2015). *Towards an autonomic auto-scaling prediction system for cloud resource provisioning.*

13. M. Barati and S. Sharifian. (2015). *A hybrid heuristic-based tuned support vector regression model for cloud load prediction.*

14. P. Padala et al. (2014). *Scaling of Cloud Applications Using Machine Learning.*

15. T. Lorido-Botran et al. (2014). *A Review of Auto-scaling Techniques for Elastic Applications in Cloud Environments.*

16. H. Alipour et al. (2014). *Analyzing auto-scaling issues in cloud environments.*

17. H. Fernandez et al. (2014). *Autoscaling Web Applications in Heterogeneous Cloud Infrastructures.*

18. N. R. Herbst et al. (2013). *Self-adaptive workload classification and forecasting for proactive resource provisioning.*

19. E. Barrett et al. (2012). *Applying reinforcement learning towards automating resource allocation and application scalability in the cloud.*

20. D. Villegas et al. (2012). *An analysis of provisioning and allocation policies for infrastructure-as-a-service clouds.*

21. S. Islam et al. (2012). *How a consumer can measure elasticity for cloud platforms.*

22. — (2012). *Empirical Prediction Models for Adaptive Resource Provisioning in the Cloud.*

23. R. Han et al. (2012). *Lightweight Resource Scaling for Cloud Applications.*

24. X. Dutreilh et al. (2011). *Using Reinforcement Learning for Autonomic Resource Allocation in Clouds: towards a fully automated workflow.*

25. N. Roy et al. (2011). *Efficient Autoscaling in the Cloud Using Predictive Models for Workload Forecasting.*

26. W. Iqbal et al. (2011). *Adaptive resource provisioning for read intensive multi-tier applications in the cloud.*

27. M. Mao and M. Humphrey. (2011). *Auto-scaling to minimize cost and meet application deadlines in cloud workflows.*

28. Nilabja Roy et al. (2011). *Efficient Autoscaling in the Cloud Using Predictive Models for Workload Forecasting.*

29. Zhiming Shen et al. (2011). *Cloudscale: Elastic resource scaling for multi-tenant cloud systems.*

30. P. Lama and X. Zhou. (2010). *Autonomic Provisioning with Self-Adaptive Neural Fuzzy Control for End-to-end Delay Guarantee.*

31. E. Caron et al. (2010). *Forecasting for Cloud computing on-demand resources based on pattern matching.*

32. Z. Gong et al. (2010). *PRESS: PRedictive elastic resource scaling for cloud systems.*

33. S. Meng et al. (2010). *Tide: Achieving self-scaling in virtualized datacenter management middleware.*

34. S. Yi et al. (2010). *Reducing Costs of Spot Instances via Checkpointing in the Amazon Elastic Compute Cloud.*

35. H. C. Lim et al. (2009). *Automated control in cloud computing: Challenges and opportunities.*

36. E. Kalyvianaki et al. (2009). *Self-adaptive and self-configured CPU resource provisioning for virtualized servers using Kalman filters.*

37. B. Urgaonkar et al. (2008). *Agile dynamic provisioning of multi-tier internet applications.*

Resources

1. "Delta Meltdown Reflects Problems with Aging Technology." (2016). *http://on.wsj.com/2wCcsPq*.

2. "Southwest Outage, Canceled Flights Cost an Estimated $54M." (2016). *https://bloom.bg/2wsoJp4*

3. "WhatsApp apologises as service crashes on New Year's Eve: Users worldwide unable to connect as messaging app goes offline." (2015). *http://dailym.ai/2vtE6J3*.

4. "Google Docs Outage Further Saps Friday Productivity." (2015). *http://on.wsj.com/2vtEbMR*.

5. "Slack outage cues massive freakout, but it's significant for more than that." (2015). *http://mashable.com/2015/11/23/slack-down-reactions/*.

6. "AWS Outage." (2012). *http://aws.amazon.com/message/67457/*.

7. "Twitter Is Down, Again." (2012). *http://tcrn.ch/2wK5Ihz*.

8. "Twitter Outage." (2012). *http://bit.ly/twitter-outage-2012*.

9. "Google Talk Is Down: Worldwide Outage Since 6:50 AM EDT." (2012). *http://tcrn.ch/2vjNIqH*.

10. "AWS Outage." (2011). *http://aws.amazon.com/message/65648/*.

11. "Twitter Outage." (2011). *http://status.twitter.com/post/2369720246/streaming-outage*.

12. "Time is Money: The Value of On-Demand." by Joe Weinman (2011). *http://joeweinman.com/Resources/Joe_Weinman_Time_Is_Money.pdf*

13. "Lightning Strike Triggers Amazon EC2 Outage." (2009). *http://www.datacenterknowledge.com/archives/2009/06/11/lightning-strike-triggers-amazon-ec2-outage/*.

14. "Outage for Amazon Web Services." (2009). *http://www.datacenterknowledge.com/archives/2009/07/19/outage-for-amazon-web-services/*.

15. "Brief Power Outage for Amazon Data Center." (Dec. 2009). *http://www.datacenterknowledge.com/archives/2009/12/10/power-outage-for-amazon-data-center/*.

16. "Major Outage for Amazon S3 and EC2." (Feb. 2008). *http://www.datacenterknowledge.com/archives/2008/02/15/major-outage-for-amazon-s3-and-ec2/*.

17. "Amazon EC2 Outage Wipes Out Data." (Oct. 2007). *http://www.datacenterknowledge.com/archives/2007/10/02/amazon-ec2-outage-wipes-out-data/*.

18. "List of web host service outages." *http://bit.ly/list-host-outages*.

Virtualization

AMONG OTHERS, TWO GOALS OF CAPACITY PLANNING ARE TO EMPLOY THE resources that your organization has at hand in the most efficient manner, and to predict future needs based on the patterns of current use. For well-defined workloads, you potentially can get pretty close to utilizing most of the hardware resources for each class of server you have, such as databases, web servers, and storage devices. Unfortunately, web application workloads are rarely (if ever) perfectly aligned with the available hardware resources.

"Don't worry, the expectations
are the same as ever ... only
completely different."

In such circumstances, you end up with inefficiencies in usage of available capacity. For example, if you know that a database's specific ceiling (limit) is determined by its memory or disk usage, but meanwhile it uses very little CPU, there's no reason to buy servers with two quad-core CPUs. That resource (and investment) will simply be wasted unless you direct the server to work on other CPU-intensive tasks. Even buying a single CPU can be overkill. But often, that's all that's available, so you end up with idle resources. It's the continual need to balance correct resources to workload demand that makes capacity planning so important, and in recent years some technologies and approaches have emerged that render this balance easier to manage, with ever-finer granularity.

Overview

There are many definitions of virtualization. In general, virtualization is the abstraction of computing resources at various levels of a computer. Hardware, application, and operating system (OS) levels are some of the few places in which this abstraction can take place, but in the context of growing web operations, virtualization is generally used to describe OS abstraction, otherwise known as *server virtualization*. Examples include the Xen[1] virtual machine (VM) monitor, VMWare's ESXi[2] server, the Hyper-V (*https://www.microsoft.com/en-us/cloud-platform/server-virtualization*), and KVM (*http://www.linux-kvm.org/page/Main_Page*), in which a host OS functions with the hypervisor running on top of it. Because a VM is not dependent on the state of the physical hardware, you can install multiple VMs on a single set of hardware. Entire books are written on the topic of virtualization. As it relates to capacity planning, virtualization allows for more granular control of how resources are used at the *bare metal* level. Here are some of the advantages of virtualization:

Efficient use of resources
> There's no reason to waste an entire server to run small tasks like corporate email. If there are spare CPU, memory, or disk resources, you can pile on other services to that resource to make better use of it. Because of this, organizations use virtualization to consolidate many servers to run on a single piece of hardware.

Portability and fault tolerance
> When a physical host is reaching known (or perhaps unknown) limits, or suffers a hardware failure, a guest OS (and its associated load) can be safely migrated to another host.

---

1 P. Barham et al. (2003). *Xen and the Art of Virtualization.*
2 E. Haletky. (2011). *VMware ESX and ESXi in the Enterprise: Planning Deployment of Virtualization Servers.*

Development sandboxes

Because entire operating systems can be created and destroyed without harming the underlying host environment, virtualization is ideal for building multiple development environments that demand different operating systems, kernels, or system configurations. If there's a major bug that causes the entire test-bed to explode, no problem—you can easily re-create it.

Less management overhead

Virtualization makes it possible for you to consolidate several individual servers with idle resources into fewer servers with higher resource utilization. This can translate into reduced power consumption as well as a smaller datacenter footprint. Another benefit of less hardware is that there are fewer parts subject to failure, such as disk drives, CPUs, and power supplies. Of course, the counterpoint to this is consolidation can increase the exposure to a single-point-of-failure (SPOF), given that many services are dependent on the same physical hardware. Virtualization packages solve this potential problem by allowing VMs to easily migrate from server to server for disaster recovery, and for rebalancing workloads.

Virtualization essentially allows you to do more work with less hardware. These efficiencies have a trade-off in that they can complicate measurements. Identifying which resource is virtual usage and which is physical can be confusing, as the abstraction layer introduces another level of metric collection and measurement. One additional advantage to virtualization is that you can separate application ceilings on a role-by-role basis, even when you are only running on a single physical server. For example, suppose that you are consolidating email, backup, and logging services onto a single server. You might allocate more memory to the logging services for buffering the log writes to disk, and you might allocate more disk space to the backup application so it has room to grow. As long as you can keep track of the virtual and the physical, the capacity planning process is roughly the same. Consider the physical servers as generic containers in which you can run a limited number of virtual servers.

In recent years, containers have emerged as an alternative to VMs. Containers encapsulate an application with its dependencies. Containers share resources with the host OS and hence are very efficient. Further, containers can be started and stopped very quickly. The portability of containers can potentially help eliminate bugs induced due to change in the environment. Thus, the use of containers enables developers to build software locally, knowing that it will run identically regardless of the host environment.

───── NOTE ─────

For a comparative performance evaluation of VMs and Linux containers, read the 2014 paper titled "An Updated Performance Comparison of Virtual Machines and Linux Containers (*http://ieeexplore.ieee.org/document/7095802*)," by W. Felter et al.

Figure A-1 illustrates three applications running in three separate VMs on a host. The hypervisor creates and runs VMs, controls access to the underlying OS and hardware, and interprets system calls when necessary. Each VM requires a full copy of the OS, the application being run, and any supporting libraries. In contrast, Figure A-1 illustrates three applications running in a containerized system. Unlike VMs, the host kernel is shared between the different containers. Akin to a hypervisor on a VM, the container engine is responsible for starting and stopping containers. Processes running in containers are equivalent to native processes on the host and do not incur the overhead associated with hypervisor execution.

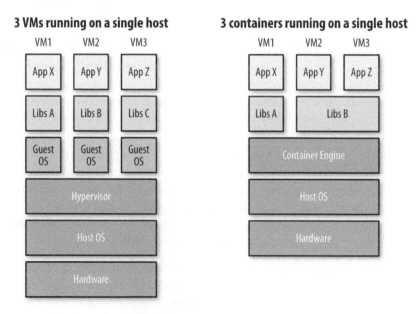

Figure A-1. *(a) Three VMs running on a single host (b) Three containers running on a single host*

There are two sides of a coin. Alongside the benefits outlined earlier, there are challenges associated with the use of VMs and containers on public clouds; for instance, security and performance isolation. The latter is, in part, addressed by the use of dedicated instances; however, the use dedicated instances limits the benefits of the pay-per-usage model of the cloud. The performance of instances on the cloud can vary to a great extent. We can ascribe this, in part, to the following:

- Datacenters grow to contain multiple generations of hardware (e.g., network switches, disks, and CPU architectures) as old components are replaced or new capacity is added. In a 2012 paper titled "Exploiting Hardware Heterogeneity within the Same Instance Type of Amazon EC2" by Z. Ou et al., the authors reported that Amazon EC2 uses diversified hardware to host the same type of instance. The hardware diversity results in performance variation. In general, the variation between the fast instances and slow instances can reach 40 percent. In some applications, the variation can even approach up to 60 percent.

- Network topology can vary, with some routes having lower latency or supporting higher bandwidth than others.

- Multiplexing systems across customers with different workloads also can lead to uneven resource contention across the cloud.

For further reading about performance variability in the cloud, refer to the following:

1. B. Guenter et al. (2011). *Managing Cost, Performance, and Reliability Tradeoffs for Energy-Aware Server Provisioning*.

2. V. Jalaparti et al. (2012). *Bridging the Tenant-Provider Gap in Cloud Services*.

3. B. Farley et al. (2012). *More for Your Money: Exploiting Performance Heterogeneity in Public Clouds*.

4. Z. Ou et al. (2013). *Is the Same Instance Type Created Equal? Exploiting Heterogeneity of Public Clouds*.

5. P. Leitner and J. Cito, (2014). *Patterns in the Chaos - a Study of Performance Variation and Predictability in Public IaaS Clouds*.

6. J. Mogul and R. R. Kompella, (2015). *Inferring the Network Latency Requirements of Cloud Tenants*.

7. A. Anwar et al. (2016). *Towards Managing Variability in the Cloud*.

Looking Back and Moving forward

Virtualization technologies have spawned an entire industry of computing "utility" providers who take advantage of the efficiencies inherent in virtualization to build *public clouds*. Cloud service providers then make those resources available on a cost-per-usage basis via an API, or other means. Because cloud computing and storage essentially takes some of the infrastructure deployment and management out of the hands of the developer, using a cloud infrastructure can be an attractive alternative to running one's own servers. Cloud infrastructure providers offer a "menu" of compute instance items, ranging from lower-powered CPU and memory platforms to large-scale, multicore CPU systems (nowadays, even graphics processing units [GPUs] and field-programmable gate arrays [FPGAs] also are supported) with massive amounts of memory. These choices aren't as customizable as off-the-shelf systems you own; so, when you need to, determine how to fit the needs using the "menu." Since the writing of the first edition of this book, public clouds such as Amazon Web Services (AWS) and Microsoft Azure have grown to businesses of more than $10 billion.

Note that virtualization has been researched for more than four decades. Early research in virtualization can be traced back to the following:

1. R. F. Rosin. (1969). *Contemporary Concepts of Microprogramming and Emulation.*

2. R. P. Goldberg. (1973). *Architecture of Virtual Machines.*

3. R. P. Goldberg. (1974). *Survey of Virtual Machine Research.*

4. G. J. Popek and R. P. Goldberg. (1974). *Formal Requirements for Virtualizable Third-Generation Architectures.*

5. L. Seawright and R. MacKinnon. (1979). *VM/370—A Study of Multiplicity and Usefulness.*

6. P. H. Gum. (1983). *System/370 Extended Architecture: Facilities for Virtual Machines.*

At one time, computers were seen as equipment only managed by large financial, educational, or research institutions. Because computers were extremely expensive, IBM and other manufacturers built large-scale minicomputers and mainframes to handle processing for multiple users at once, utilizing many of the virtualization concepts still in use today. Users would be granted slices of computation time from mainframe machines, accessing them from *thin*, or *dumb*, terminals. Users submitted jobs whose computation contended for resources. The centralized system was managed via queues, virtual operating systems, and system accounting that governed resource allocation. All of the heavy lifting of computation was handled by the mainframe and its operators, and was largely invisible to the end users. The design of these systems was largely driven by security and reliability, so considerable effort was applied to containing user environments and data redundancy. Virtualization gained traction in datacenter space and then became the bedrock of innovation in the realm of cloud computing. For a deeper dive into datacenter virtualization, refer to the following:

1. C. Guo et al. (2010) *SecondNet: A Data Center Network Virtualization Architecture with Bandwidth Guarantees.*

2. G. A. A. Santana. (2013). *Data Center Virtualization Fundamentals: Understanding Techniques and Designs for Highly Efficient Data Centers with Cisco Nexus, UCS, MDS, and Beyond.*

Today, virtualization is not limited to compute, it also is applied to network, storage, and I/O. To mitigate the impact of virtualization on performance, there's been increasing support for virtualization in hardware. Last but not least, security in the context of virtualization has also been an active area of research. To learn more about the various facets of virtualization, refer to the following research papers and surveys:

1. T. Clark. (2005). *Storage Virtualization: Technologies for Simplifying Data Storage and Management.*

2. K. Adams and O. Agesen. (2006). *A comparison of software and hardware techniques for x86 virtualization.*

3. S. Crosby and D. Brown. (2006). *The Virtualization Reality: Are hypervisors the new foundation for system software?*

4. K. Roussos. (2007). *Storage Virtualization Gets Smart.*

5. S. Rixner. (2008). *Network Virtualization: Breaking the Performance Barrier.*

6. M. Carbone et al. (2008). *Taming Virtualization.*

7. X. Chen et al. (2008). *Overshadow: a virtualization-based approach to retrofitting protection in commodity operating systems.*

8. J. Carapinha and J. Jiménez. (2009). *Network virtualization: a view from the bottom.*

9. A. van Cleeff et al. (2009). *Security Implications of Virtualization: A Literature Study.*

10. M. Rosenblum and C. Waldspurger. (2012). *I/O Virtualization.*

11. M. Pearce et al. (2013). *Virtualization: Issues, security threats, and solutions.*

12. G. Pék et al. (2013). *A survey of security issues in hardware virtualization.*

13. T. Koponen et al. (2014). *Network virtualization in multi-tenant datacenters.*

14. J. Shuja et al. (2016). *A Survey of Mobile Device Virtualization: Taxonomy and State of the Art.*

15. Open vSwitch, [online]. Available at *http://openvswitch.org/.*

Dealing with Instantaneous Growth

Sometimes, events occur beyond our control, foresight, and budget. An unexpected incident—technological or otherwise—can wipe out all of our future projections. There are no magic theories or formulas to banish the capacity woes in these situations, but you might be able to lessen the pain.

Besides catastrophes—like a tornado destroying a datacenter—the biggest problem you are likely to face is too much traffic. Ironically, becoming more popular than you can handle could be the worst web operations nightmare that you have ever experienced. You might be fortunate enough to have a popular piece of content that is the target of links from all over the planet, or launch a new killer feature that draws more attention than you ever planned. This can be as exciting as having your name in lights, but you might not feel so fortunate at the time it's all happening.

From a capacity point of view, you can't do much instantaneously. If you are being hosted in a public cloud, it's possible to add capacity *relatively* quickly depending on how it will be used—but this approach has limits. Adding servers can only solve the "I need more servers" problem. It can't solve the more difficult architectural problems that can pop up when you least expect them.

It's not uncommon to find that edge-use cases arise (probably more often than routine capacity issues!) that tax the infrastructure in ways that you hadn't expected. For example, back at Flickr, a user had automated his webcam to take a photo of his backyard, upload it to Flickr, and tag it with the Unix timestamp *every minute* of *every day*. This makes for interesting database side effects, because it wasn't expected that it would have to generate that many unique tags for so many photos. Further, there were users who had very few photos but many *thousands* of tags on each one. Each one of these cases shed light on the limits of the database.

Mitigating Failure

The following tips and tricks are for worst-case scenarios, when other options for increasing capacity are exhausted, and substantially changing the infrastructure itself is impossible for the moment. It should be said that this type of firefighting scenario is most of what capacity planning aims to avoid; yet sometimes it's simply unavoidable. These tips and tricks aren't meant to be exhaustive—just a few things that can help when the torrent of traffic comes and the servers are dying under load.

Graceful Degradation and Disabling Heavy Features

One contingency is to disable some of the site's heavier features. Building in the ability to turn certain features on or off can help capacity and operations respond significantly, even in the absence of some massive traffic event. Having a quick, one-line configuration parameter in the application with values of *on* or *off* can be of enormous value, particularly when that feature is either the cause of a problem or contributing to unacceptable performance. For example, you can have the web servers perform geographic (country) lookups based on client IP addresses for logged-out users in an effort to deduce their language preferences. It's an operation that enhances the user experience, but it is yet another function the application must handle. Back at Flickr, after the launch of the localized version of the service in seven different languages, the aforementioned feature was turned on with the launch. It almost immediately placed too much load on the mechanisms that carried out the country lookups. The problem turned out to be an artificial throttle placed on the rate of requests the geo server could handle, which was tuned too conservatively. The issue was isolated and fixed by lifting the throttle to a more acceptable level and then turned the feature (which is mostly transparent) back on. Had a quick on/off switch not been implemented for that feature—in other words, if it had been hardcoded within the application—it would have taken more time to troubleshoot, disable, and fix. During this time, the site would have been in a degraded state, or possibly even down.

Ideally, you should work with the various products, development, design, and operations groups to identify an agreed upon set of features to which you can apply on/off switches. When faced with a choice between having the full site go down and operating it with a reduced set of features, it's sometimes easy to compromise. This is particularly important in domains such as ecommerce for which there's immediate impact to the bottom line.

Here's an anecdotal example: a large news organization was serving web pages with the tallied results of a United States presidential election. Its web servers were running close to capacity all day. On the night of the election, traffic overwhelmed the organization. It had no spare servers to add quickly, and the website began crumbling, serving broken images, and some pages with images but no other content. The decision was quickly made to stop logging. Now remember, this was before any large-scale traffic counting services were available, and all traffic metrics for ad serving were taken from the logs written by the origin servers themselves, audited alongside any ad-serving logs. By disabling logging, the site could continue and buy some time to assemble more equipment to handle the load. For hours, the site went without any concrete way to measure how much traffic it received, on what was certainly its busiest traffic day up until that point. The decision to stop logging all traffic was the correct one. The relief on the disk systems was enough to allow the servers to recover and serve the rest of the traffic spike, which lasted into the early hours of the next day.

Likewise, at Netflix, at times, personalization of recommendations was foregone and generic recommendations were served in the interest of better response time. Today, most websites use a wide variety of third-party services for, say, advertising, analytics, social media presence, and so on. In times of stress, you can turn off one or more of these third-party services, given that they are not core to the user experience.

Baked Static Pages and Beyond

Another technique frequently employed by sites that encounter heavy and erratic traffic is to convert a dynamic page to a static HTML page. This can be either terribly difficult or very easy, depending on how dynamic the page is originally—increasingly, with today's websites, a large percentage of client time is spent executing JavaScript code. You can gain some safety by building static pages for only the most popular and least dynamic pages.

Converting pages from dynamic to static is called *baking* a web page. An example of how this can work well is using a news page showing recent photos that one updates every two or three hours. Under normal conditions, the obvious design is to create a dynamic page that reads in the photos of the hour from a database or other content management system. Under duress, you could hardcode the image URLs into the page and change them manually as needed.

Baking a page into static HTML clearly breaks a lot of functionality found in today's more dynamic websites, but static pages come with some operational advantages:

- They don't initiate database lookups.
- They can be served very fast. Static content can display up to 10 times faster than dynamic pages that must wait for other backend services.
- They are easy to cache. If you need even more speed, you can cache static pages quite easily via reverse-proxy caching. This, of course, can introduce an entire new layer of complexity, but if you are already using caching for other parts of a site, it can be easily implemented.

The disadvantages of baking static HTML pages under duress are also worth noting:

- You need a framework in which to bake and rebake those pages quickly and easily. Ideally, you should have a single command or button on a web page that will replace the original dynamic page with the static HTML replacement, and also reverse the operation. This takes some time and effort to develop.

- You need to track what is where so that when changes do happen, you can propagate them. The generation of the static content should be synchronized with the content origin (usually a database). If changes are made to the database, those changes must be reflected (rebaked) to all of the static pages that include the content.

Beyond static pages, you can employ many other approaches to minimize the impact on user experience during times of high traffic. For instance, you can substitute high-resolution images with low-resolution images. In a similar vein, you can substitute 8 K UHD/4 K UHD video with HD video.

---- NOTE --

For more information, read *High Performance Images: Shrink, Load, and Deliver Images for Speed* by C. Bendell et al. (O'Reilly) as well as the paper titled "Image Optimization" (*http://bit.ly/grigorik-image-opt*) by I. Grigorik.

Cache but Serve Stale

Caching is used in many different components within backend infrastructures. Caching frequently requested objects from clients (or other backend server layers) can have a significantly positive effect on performance and scalability but also requires careful deployment and increases the cost of management. Normally, caching done this way *accelerates* content delivery, and the *freshness* of each cached object is controlled and monitored by headers that can indicate the age of an object and how long it's desirable to serve the cached version of it.

As an extension to baking pages, and to take more advantage of caching, you can relax the content's freshness requirements. This is usually a lot easier than building static pages where there were none before, but it involves more complexities. In the context of images and videos, t he use of Content Delivery Networks (CDNs)—which are typically distributed around the globe—has become a norm. This reduces response time by obviating the need to pull content from the origin server. CDNs also purge (remove and update) content constantly so that fresh content is delivered. At Netflix, the use of a CDN was key to minimizing buffering when a subscriber streamed a video. Likewise, at Twitter, the use of a CDN was key to ensuring fast delivery of photos and videos in tweets.

Handling Outages

When failure comes knocking at the door (and sadly, it will at some point), there are a number of steps that you can take to minimize the pain for the users, as well. Good customer service requires strong and effective communications between the operations and customer care groups, so users are promptly informed about site outage and problems such as bugs, capacity, and performance. We thought to share some of the lessons we've learned when serving such a strong and vocal online community during emergencies or outages. If a kitchen is flooded, but a plumber is underneath the sink, you at least have the feeling that someone has recognized the problem and is trying to resolve it. A good plumber will give updates on the cause of the problem and what must be done to fix it.

Web applications are different: you can't see someone working on a problem, and users can sometimes feel left in the dark. Our experience has been that users are much more forgiving of problems when you keep them in the information loop. To this end, you should set up forums in which users can report bugs and issues and a blog (hosted outside of your own datacenter so that it can't be affected by outages) where the service provider can post updates on what's going on if the site or app is down. In addition, nowadays, updates are also posted on Twitter.

An entire book can be written on the topic of customer care for online communities. Unfortunately, this isn't that book. But from a web operations perspective, site outages can—and do—happen. How your organization handles them is just as important as how long it takes to get back up and running.

Capacity Tools

MEASUREMENT, MONITORING, AND MANAGEMENT TOOLS INFORM AND GUIDE
your capacity plan. In this appendix, we've compiled a list of some of the more popular tools and utilities for reference.

Monitoring

As we discussed in Chapter 3, there can be a lot of overlap in event notification software (tools that alert on resources based on thresholds) and metric collection and display tools. Some of the following tools have alerting abilities, some of them are more focused on graphing and collection, and some have both.

Metric Collection and Event Notification Systems

- DataDog (*http://www.datadog.com/*)
- Opsclarity (*http://www.opsclarity.com/*)
- Prometheus (*http://www.prometheus.io/*)
- CoScale (*http://www.coscale.com/*)
- Signalfx (*http://www.signalfx.com/*)
- SignalSciences (*http://www.signalsciences.com/*)
- Ganglia (*http://ganglia.info/*)

Born out of the high-performance computing (HPC) community, Ganglia has a very active community of users and developers. We use Ganglia extensively at Flickr, as do Wikipedia and other large-scale social networking sites.

- Nagios (*http://nagios.org/*)

- Cacti (*http://cacti.net/*)

- Zabbix (*http://zabbix.com/*)

- Hyperic HQ (*http://hyperic-hq.sourceforge.net/*)

- Munin (*http://munin-monitoring.org/*)

- ZenOSS (*http://www.zenoss.com/*)

- OpenNMS (*http://opennms.org/*)

- GroundWork (*http://www.gwos.com/*) (GroundWork is a hybrid of Nagios and Ganglia)

- Monit (*http://www.mmonit.com/monit*)

Ad Hoc Measurement and Graphing Tools

RRDTool (http://oss.oetiker.ch/rrdtool/)
Mature graphing and metric storage tool.

Collectd (http://collectd.org/)
Scalable system stats collection daemon. Uses multicast, like Ganglia.

Rrd2csv (https://wiki.opennms.org/wiki/Rrd2csv)
RRD to CSV converter.

Dstat (http://dag.wieers.com/home-made/dstat/)
System statistics tool, modular.

GraphClick (http://www.arizona-software.ch/graphclick/)
Digitizer that constructs data from an image of a graph—handy when you have the image but not the raw data.

Netflix Servo (https://github.com/Netflix/servo)
Provides an interface for exposing and publishing application metrics in Java.

Java Performance

- VisualVM (*http://visualvm.java.net/*)

- GCViewer (*http://www.tagtraum.com/gcviewer.html*)

- JProfiler (*https://www.ej-technologies.com/products/jprofiler/overview.html*)

- JProbe (*https://docs.oracle.com/cd/E19501-01/819-3659/beafr/index.html*)
- Java Interactive Profiler (*http://jiprof.sourceforge.net/*)
- Profiler4j (*http://profiler4j.sourceforge.net/*)

Netflix Vector (https://github.com/Netflix/vector)
   On-host performance monitoring framework.

Deployment Tools

In this section, we look at tools for automating OS installation, configuration, and cluster management. In addition, we list tools available for inventory management, trend analysis, and curve fitting.

Automated OS Installation

SystemImager (http://wiki.systemimager.org/)
   SystemImager comes from the HPC community and is used to install thousand-node computer clusters. Used by many large-scale web operations, as well. Interesting work has been done to use bitTorrent as the transfer mechanism.

FAI (http://www.informatik.uni-koeln.de/fai)
   A Debian autoinstallation tool with a healthy community.

KickStart (http://fedoraproject.org/wiki/Anaconda/Kickstart/)

Cobbler (http://cobbler.et.redhat.com/)
   Cobbler is a relatively new project from RedHat, supporting RedHat, Fedora, and CentOs.

Configuration Management

Chef (http://chef.io/)

Puppet (http://reductivelabs.com/trac/puppet)
   Fast becoming a very popular configuration tool, Puppet has some very passionate developers and a very involved community of users. Written in Ruby.

CFEngine (http://www.cfengine.org/)
   Written in C, it's been around for many years and has a large installed base and active community.

Bcfg2 (http://bcfg2.org/)

Lcfg (http://www.lcfg.org/) (Large-scale Unix configuration system)

Cluster Management/Container Orchestration

Capistrano (http://www.capify.org/)
Written in Ruby, Capistrano is becoming popular in the Rails environments.

Dsh (http://freshmeat.net/projects/dsh/)

Fabric (http://savannah.nongnu.org/projects/fab)

Func (https://fedorahosted.org/func/)
Func is the Fedora Unified Network Controller, and can replace ad hoc cluster-wide ssh commands with an authenticated client/server architecture.

XCat (http://xcat.sourceforge.net/)

Kubernetes (http://kubernetes.io/)

Mesosphere Marathon (http://mesosphere.github.io/marathon)

Docker Swarm (https://www.docker.com/products/docker-swarm)

CoreOs Fleet (https://coreos.com/fleet/)

Inventory Management

iClassify (https://wiki.hjksolutions.com/display/IC/Home)

OCS Inventory NG (http://www.ocsinventory-ng.org/)

Trend Analysis and Curve Fitting

Fityk (http://www.unipress.waw.pl/fityk/)

SciPy (http://www.scipy.org/)

R (http://www.r-project.org/)

Books on Queuing Theory and the Mathematics of Capacity Planning

1. Leonard Kleinrock. (1975). *Queueing Systems. Volume 1: Theory* (1st ed.).

2. __ (1976). *Queueing Systems. Volume 2: Computer Applications* (1st ed.).

3. R. Jain. (1991). *The Art of Computer Systems Performance Analysis: Techniques for Experimental Design, Measurement, Simulation, and Modeling.*

4. D. A. Menascé and V. A. F. Almeida. (2000). *Scaling for E-business.* Prentice Hall.

5. __ (2001). *Capacity Planning For Web Services: Metrics, Models, and Methods.* Prentice Hall.

6. D. A. Menascé et al. (2004). *Performance By Design*. Prentice Hall.

7. N. Gunther. (2006). *Guerilla Capacity Planning*. Springer.

Index

B

considerations for multiple datacenters, 129

moving window of forecasts, 132

reviewing forecasts for accuracy, 131

Fowler, Martin, 1

G

Ganglia, 51, 54, 200

collecting and plotting disk utilization for database, 77

goals

determining goal for capacity planning, 11

setting for capacity, 25-44

gold client image, 142

Goldratt, E.M., 11, 15

Google Preemptible VMs, 160

graceful degradation, 192

setting up without affecting high-level goal, 13

graphics processing units (GPUs), 141, 187

graphing tools, 200

Graphite, 51

growth

instantaneous, dealing with, 192-197

handling outages, 196

mitigating failure, 192-196

support for, in capacity planning, 11

H

hard disk drives, 62

metrics comparing performance of, 63

metrics on disk utilization and throughput, 67

Hard Disk Sentinel tool, 64

hardware

becoming cheaper and faster, 104

centralized configuration and management environment, 139

decisions on, vertical, horizontal, and diagonal scaling, 39-42

diversity of hardware on public clouds, 186

homogenizing to prevent headaches, 140

inventory management for, 148

not buying enough versus too much, 4

resource ceilings, 39

hardware VM (HVM), 144

HDDs (see hard disk drives)

high availability, 31

historical data, 133

horizontal scaling, 6, 40

HTTP server service, 149

Httperf, 74, 88

human attention span, 2

HVM (hardware VM) AMIs, 144

I

iClassify, 148

imaging new machines, 142

infrastructure as code, 137

infrastructure monitoring services, 51

infrastructure, assessing current working of, 4

innovation, increasing rate of, 15

Instagram, user base and traffic, 33

installation tools, automated, 137, 141-147, 201

installation process, 146

preparing an OS image, 145

instance types

GPU-based, 141

with field-programmable gate arrays (FPGAs), 141

intent of users, 28

interaction of users with content, 29

inventory management, 148

tools for, 202

IOBench, 64

J

just-in-time (JIT) inventory, 124-126

L

LAMP (Linux, Apache, MySQL, and PHP) stack, 7, 53

latency and throughput, tradeoff between, 163

least connections load balancing, 60

least recently used (LRU) cache eviction algorithm, 83

    reference age, 84

Linux

    Amazon machine images (AMIs), 143

    monitoring utilities, 46

load balancers, 59-61

    benefits of using, 74

    connection draining, 157

load balancing

    algorithms used for, 59

    finding web server ceilings in load-balancing environment, 70-73

load testing, 51

    artificial load testing, limitations of, 74

    latency and throughput, tradeoff between, 163

    production load testing with a single machine, 73

logging, aggregated configuration and management logging system, 138

logs

    storage consumption by, 67

    treating as past metrics, 55

long-term data storage, 66

LRU (see least recently used cache eviction algorithm)

M

Maglev load balancer, 60

MAMP (Mac, Apache, MySQL, PHP) stack, 53

master-slave database architecture, 79

MEAN (MongoDB, Express.js, Angular.js, Node.js) stack, 53

mean time to resolution (MTTR), 35

measurements, 11, 46-100

    API usage and effect on capacity, 94-97

    applications of monitoring, 61-94

        application-level measurement, 61

        caching systems, 80-84

        database capacity, 75-80

        establishing caching system ceilings, 84-90

        speccial use and multiple use servers, 90-94

        storage capacity, 62-74

    capacity tracking tools, 51-61

        fundamentals and elements of metric collection systems, 52

        Ganglia, 54

        monitoring as tool for urgent problem identification, 55

        network measurement and planning, 57-58

        round-robin database and RRDTool, 53

        SNMP, 55

        treating logs as past metrics, 55

    deciding which metrics to measure and follow, 49

    examples and reality, 97

    of system resources, observer effect, 50

    tools for, 199, 200

    tools for, desired capabilities, 48

    usefulness in recognizing trends, 105

Memcached, 84, 127

service level agreements (SLAs), 30-32

    user expectations, 33-35

resources

    installation and management after procurement, 4

    resource ceilings, 38

RESTful web APIs, 3

revenue

    equating downtime to lost revenue, 31

roles

    defining, 148

    splitting web server roles to serve dynamic or static content, 149

    web server role, 149

round-robin database (RRD), 53

    and RRDTool, 53

RPS (see requests per second)

RRDTool, 54

RUM, real user monitoring, 52

S

safety factors in web operations, 122

SAS (Serial Attached SCSI) hard disk drives, 63

SATA protocol hard disks, 62

scalability analysis, 163

scaling

    artificial (or load testing), 51

    autoscaling (see autoscaling)

    database-driven web applications, 8

    using public cloud infrastructure, 6

    vertical, horizontal, and diagonal scaling for hardware, 39-42

Scheduled Scaling (on AWS), 161

schemas (database), optimization of, 75

SCSI (Serial Computer System Interface) hard disk drives, 63

search, different intents of users, 28

seasonal or holiday variations, 133

server virtualization, 184

serverless architectures, 1

    implications for capacity planning, 7

servers

    comparing server architectures, 42

    production load testing with a single machine, 73

    resource ceilings, 39

    serving more traffic with fewer servers, 42

    special use and multiple use, capacity measurements in, 90, 94

service level agreements (SLAs), 30-32

service-oriented architectures (SOAs), 1

    autoscaling in, 179

    determining causes of slowness in, 35

    for large-scale internet services, 7

services

    defining, 148

    SLAs placing limits on, 30

    splitting into dynamic and static htttp services, 149

    use of third-party vendors for key services, 35

    web server role and associated services, 149

shared-nothing architectures, horizontal scaling and, 40

Siege, 88

Simple Network Management Protocol (SNMP), 55

single point of failure, 40

single-server web application architecture, 36

SLAs (see service level agreements)

smartphones, generations of, variations around the world, 27

SNMP (Simple Network Management Protocol), 55

social media

effects of social websites and open APIs, 20-21

user base and traffic, 32

virality of, effects on capacity planning, 2

software, functionality moving from hardware to, 5

software-defined networking (SDN), 5

Solaris Jumpstart, 142

solid-state drives (SSDs), 63

Splunk, 55

SPOF (see single point of failure)

Spot instances, market for in public clouds, 157

Squid, 84

real-world example, cache measurement, 85-90

startup time aware autoscaling, 170-176

statistics, 11

(see also measurements; metrics)

making system stats tell stories, 8-15

statistical fluctuations in your system, 13

storage

limits on, 30

long-term data storage, 66

setting up retention period to contain costs, 54

storage capacity, 62-75

consumption rates, 64

logs and backup, metacapacity issue, 67

real-world example, tracking consumption, 65-67

storage I/O patterns, 67

Storage-Area Network (SAN), 67

synthetic monitoring, 52

system statistics

for a server, 36

measuring, 11

tying application level metrics to, database example, 111-114

SystemImager, 142, 146

U

upload limits, 30

uptime percentages, 31

user engagement, 130

user expectations, 33-35

User Timing "Standard Mark Names", 34

users

artificial end user interaction measurement, 52

delivering the best end-user experience, 11

simulation of human users by external monitoring services, 28

user management and access control, 150

V

Varnish, 84

version control for configurations, 138

vertical scaling, 40

virtual machines (VMs)

containers as alternative to, 185

monitoring tools, 48

use of VM versus container instances, 7

virtualization, 184-190

containers as alternatives to VMs, 185

homogenization of hardware in, 141

Linux AMIs, parairtual (PV) or hardware VM (HVM), 144

looking back and moving forward, 187

overview, 184

W

wait time, unexpected, determining cause of, 29

web applications

architecture of typical modern app, 3

characteristics of, evolution on onging basis, 12

database-driven, expanding, 8

web browsers, caching in, 29

web servers

finding ceilings in load-balancing environment, 70-73

forecasting peak-driven resource usage, example, 114-118

measuring capacity demands on, 38

measuring load on, 68

real-world example, 68-70

production load testing with a single machine, 73

role, example of, 149

web services

providing via open APIs, capacity management and, 21

use of, 32

websites

capacity planning for, 33

fast and highly available, designing, resourcces on, 34

performance and availability, needs for, 2

WhatsApp, user base and traffic, 32

About the Authors

Arun Kejariwal is a statistical learning principal at Machine Zone (MZ), where he leads a team of top-tier researchers working on novel techniques for install-and-click fraud detection. In addition, his team is building novel methods for bot detection, intrusion detection, and real-time anomaly detection. Arun has also worked at Twitter.

John Allspaw has spent over 20 years in software engineering and operations, and has held engineering leadership positions at Friendster, Flickr, and Etsy. He is the author of The Art of Capacity Planning and Web Operations: Keeping the Data on Time (both O'Reilly).

Colophon

The cover fonts are URW Typewriter and Guardian Sans. The text font is Adobe's Meridien; the heading font is Akzidenz-Grotesk and Adobe Minion Pro.

Learn from experts.
Find the answers you need.

Sign up for a **10-day free trial** to get **unlimited access** to all of the content on Safari, including Learning Paths, interactive tutorials, and curated playlists that draw from thousands of ebooks and training videos on a wide range of topics, including data, design, DevOps, management, business—and much more.

Start your free trial at:
oreilly.com/safari

(No credit card required.)

Milton Keynes UK
Ingram Content Group UK Ltd.
UKHW011829070824
446675UK00007B/111

9 781491 939208